"During my years in the Peace Corps, state legislature, Congress, and as a U.S. ambassador, I have developed a keen awareness of the systems that harm many populations worldwide. In the U.S., the issue of illiteracy is paramount, getting worse, and largely unaddressed. I believe that every pastor should read this book and use it as a tool for the discipleship of their congregation so they might be a blessing to the children in their community."

—Tony P. Hall, former congressman and U.S. ambassador

"America is an incredible country with a hope-inspiring dream. However, so many of our fellow citizens are unable to read at basic levels in this country and are therefore unable to participate fully in that dream. This is a crisis we can solve. *READ* is an invitation to transform this generation and all generations to come."

—John R. Kasich, former governor of Ohio

"Jeff and Tony have written a book filled with wisdom, facts, and strong reminders that following Jesus' words means reaching out to children and adults impacted by poverty. *READ* provides wisdom and guidance for mentoring and making a real difference for the most vulnerable children."

—Dr. Donna M. Beegle, President, Communication Across Barriers, Inc.

"*READ* shows readers how one healthy and encouraging adult who loves a child can set in motion social enzymes that make a real difference in some of America's most intractable civic ills. This exciting book has loads of potential if ordinary people like you and me take up its simple challenge."

—Todd Hunter, Anglican bishop and founder of the Center for Formation, Justice, and Peace

"There are few causes as unifying as childhood literacy, and few people are more well suited to make a massive dent than God's people. *READ* helps us understand *why* childhood illiteracy matters (to God and to us!) and *how* we can contribute to bringing the kingdom of heaven to earth, one book and kid at a time."

—Liz Bohannon, bestselling author and award-winning speaker, entrepreneur, and community builder

"God loves justice, and giving every child the opportunity to excel in reading is the very definition of justice. Every child deserves the same opportunities to succeed regardless of where they were born or what school they attend. *READ* is a powerful call to step up and step into the literacy gap and *do justice*!"

—Doug Kempton, founder of Soar Detroit and Lead Pastor of Grace Community Church Detroit

"The power that this book seeks to unlock may turn the world upside down. In *READ*, Tony Kriz and Jeff Martin invite us to reimagine how literacy is the power of life, liberty, justice, and love. Those who can't read need those who can to read this book with care."

—A.J. Swoboda, Ph.D., Associate Professor of Bible and Theology at Bushnell University and author of *The Gift of Thorns*

"With empirical evidence, biblical literacy, and personal anecdotes, the authors make a compelling case for Christians' responsibility in mentoring and nurturing the next generation of readers. Teaching a child to read is an act of discipleship."

—Ron Fairchild, President and CEO of Smarter Learning Group

"*READ* engages the mind with devastating illiteracy statistics, inspires the soul by calling for God's people to do justice, and moves the heart by showing how we can make a transformative difference. By dedicating one hour a week to teaching a child to read, we have the power to change their life forever."

—Reverend Roy Chang, founder and Executive Director of School Connect WA

"*READ* summons the 'people of the Book' to become champions of literacy for the millions who are never taught to read and, as a result, miss out on any decent shot at a flourishing life. I enthusiastically recommend this book for churches and individuals looking for practical, faithful action to take for the sake of those Jesus called the 'least of these.'"

—Tom Krattenmaker, author of *Confessions of a Secular Jesus Follower*

"As a Christ follower, I see that one of the greatest things we can fight for in the United States is literacy among our young kids. *READ* clearly maps out how we can get involved and make a difference."

—Ben Crane, five-time PGA Tour Champion

"Every pastor desires for their church to make a real-life difference in their local community. Few outreach initiatives have had a more transformative impact than our engagement with public schools. As a result, God's grace has allowed us to practically care for the marginalized in our city while maturing spiritually as followers of Jesus."

—Kip Jacob, Senior Pastor of SouthLake Church and founder of BeUndivided

"This book is brilliant and simple—two things that are not easily combined. With years of research, experience, wisdom, and analysis, the authors have written a book of refined truths so that we have no excuse. Sisters and brothers, take this book seriously and then *do* something about it."

—Billy Thrall, founder of Arizona CityServe and Hopefest Phoenix

"*READ* is a must-read! It illuminates the stark reality of what some people face in this unforgiving world, coupled with the surprising joy in small commitments and the unrelenting power of relationships. Even the smallest acts of kindness can change a life."

—Stephanie Korteweg, founder and Director of STARS Book Clubs

"*READ* is an invitation to Christians to rewrite the story of the childhood literacy epidemic. It's a life-changing book about a world-changing movement. This book is also a reminder that as much as these children need the church, the church needs these children. Teaching a child to read can affect eternity. And the lives we save may be our own."

—John Pattison, co-author of *Slow Church*

"The authors have crafted an inspiring and transformative guide in this one-of-a-kind book. Their profound insights and heartfelt stories illuminate the powerful impact of literacy on breaking the cycle of generational poverty. *READ* is a must-read for anyone passionate about making a tangible difference in their community."

—Tim Abare, CMO of Life Changers

READ

HOW GOD'S PEOPLE CAN BRING JUSTICE THROUGH LITERACY

BY TONY KRIZ AND JEFF MARTIN

Read
How God's People Can Bring Justice Through Literacy
© 2024 Tony Kriz and Jeff Martin

The publisher and authors support copyright and the sharing of thoughts and ideas it enables. Thank you for buying an authorized edition of this book and honoring our request to obtain permission for any use of any part of this publication, whether reproduced, transmitted in any form or by any means, electronic, mechanical, photocopying, recording, or otherwise, or stored in a retrieval system. Your honorable actions support all writers and allow the publishing industry to continue publishing books for all readers. All rights reserved.

While the publisher and author have used their best efforts in preparing this book, they make no representations or warranties with respect to the accuracy or completeness of this book and specifically disclaim any implied warranties of merchantability or fitness for a particular purpose. No warranty may be created or extended by sales representatives or written sales materials. The stories and interviews in this book are true although the names and identifiable information may have been changed to maintain confidentiality.

The publisher and author shall have neither liability nor responsibility to any person or entity with respect to loss of profit or property, damage, or injury caused or alleged to be caused directly or indirectly by the information contained in this book. The information presented herein is in no way intended as a substitute for counseling or other professional guidance.

All Bible references, except where otherwise noted, are from the New International Version (NIV) translation. Used by permission. All rights reserved.

For more information, please visit TeachAKidToRead.com

Advance Reader Copy - Not For Sale

This is an uncorrected proof. Content may change before final publication. This advance reader copy is provided for promotional purposes only and is not for resale.

Publication Date: October 15, 2024
Publisher: Aloha Publishing
ISBN (Expected): 978-1-61206-316-4

Please check any quotes against the final published version.

Printed in Canada

DEDICATION

For Grandma Gigi, who spent her life teaching young children and who made sure that my every birthday arrived with a new book full of stories of other worlds that made me want to read.

—Tony

To Liz, my beloved wife. Like the Marc Chagall print that hangs in our living room, I float around you, following your every move. I followed you to a life with Jesus . . . and when you read to children, I made it our life's work. On Halloween, the street in front of our house is full of children you've read to, lined up to say hi to Mrs. Martin— 10 years, 17 classrooms, 25 kids a class, every week from October to June. And when COVID came, you read with them one at a time. So many lives blessed . . . I can't do the math . . . but God can.

—Jeff

CONTENTS

Introduction — 23
1. Disrupting Generational Poverty — 29

Part One: It's for the Children

2. For Such a Time as This — 35
3. The Thing Tony Campolo Said — 39
4. How to Build a Brain — 43
5. Trauma — 47
6. Yoga Boy — 51
7. For I Was Hungry — 57
8. For I Was a Stranger — 61
9. For I Was Naked — 65
10. For I Was Sick — 71
11. For I Was in Prison — 75
12. Nas and Craig — 79
13. Knit Together — 83
14. "Typical" Meets "Normal" — 87
15. Self-Esteem — 91
16. The Least of These, the Reading-Mentor Edition — 95

Part Two: It's for the People of God

17. Rosie	99
18. Loving Your Neighbor	103
19. Storyteller	107
20. A Parable	111
21. Rethinking the Good Samaritan	115
22. The Thing C.S. Lewis Wrote	119
23. One	123
24. I Didn't Want to Do It	127
25. A Little About the USA	131
26. Heal Society	135
27. The Financial Impact	139
28. Poverty-Informed Mentoring	143
29. A Key to Evangelism	147
30. Formulas	151
31. Why Wouldn't I?	155

Part Three: It's for Your Church

32. A Transformational Change	161
33. We Are Book People	165
34. The Church's Literacy History	169
35. Confession	173
36. God Loves Justice	177
37. Change the World	181

38. Churches Are the Best	185
39. For Our Place and Time	189
40. Full Deployment	193
41. Grow Your Church	197
42. Other People's Money	201
43. And It Might Change Everything	205
44. Making History	209
45. Belonging	213
46. Practicing for Heaven	217
47. Follow Me	221
Conclusion	225
How to Get Involved	231
Acknowledgments	233
About the Authors	237
Endnotes	239

TEACH A CHILD TO READ,
GIVE A CHILD A CHANCE.

—PASTOR SULTAN COLE

1 IN 3 CHILDREN IN 4TH GRADE ARE BELOW THE **BASIC** READING LEVEL IN THE UNITED STATES.[1]

80% OF LOW-INCOME 4TH-GRADERS
NEVER REACH READING PROFICIENCY.[2]

60% OF YOUNG MEN ENTERING PRISON IN THE U.S. **CANNOT** READ AT A 3RD-GRADE LEVEL.[3]

130 MILLION ADULTS IN THE UNITED STATES
STRUGGLE TO READ BASIC SENTENCES.[4]

INTRODUCTION

Jeff and I were both dumb kids . . . at least that was the word people used back then. It was the word used by the kids in the schoolyard. More significantly, we said it to ourselves in our inside, secret voices.

Both of us grew up struggling to read. School was not a place we felt like we belonged and books fought us all throughout adolescence. Remedial classes and being teased on the playground were both part of any typical day.

And while all of that is true . . . this book is *not* about Jeff and me.

You see, while the struggle was real, Jeff and I were not left alone.

We were among the lucky ones. We had full stomachs and safe homes. We had supportive adults. We were surrounded by words: good words . . . big words and small words, words of affirmation, and words around the dinner table.

And in my case, I had lots and lots of words at church. For me, church was a game changer. More on that in a minute.

So who is the book about?

In the U.S., 40% of children grow up without a healthy community, a safe home, a full stomach, and a world of words. When we say a "world of words," we mean a world of books and bedtime stories, of encouragement, and of belief in a brighter future.

In the United States, 34% of 4th-graders read below the basic level.[5] It is not their fault. They may show up to school this week. When they do, their brains and bodies may not have the resources necessary to complete the reading process that came naturally to so many of us. As a child, were you convinced you would always learn to read? You might be surprised to know that many are not.

Too many children sit in classrooms that are under-resourced and where teachers are overtaxed.

In the U.S. education system, a ticking clock is placed on every child. And that clock's alarm goes off at age 10. Our system gives children until about age 10 to *learn* to read . . . and then, from that day forward, they are expected to *read* to learn. There are no more public resources to help them.

If a child is not surrounded by other support systems, like Jeff and I experienced, where are they to turn? They will fall further and further behind. They will drop out. They will fall through the cracks of society.

These children, these often-forgotten children, ignored by society and sentenced to devastation, will in many ways be the subject of this book . . .

. . . but this book is ultimately *not* about the children either.

Growing up, church was my second home and at least three times a week I found myself running through the halls of that old brick building in downtown Eugene, Oregon, bumping into unending family, friends, Sunday school teachers, and pastors. Every one of those beautiful adults was committed to my future. And though inside I was "dumb," outside all I heard was, "Tony, we believe in you."

Jeff came to faith after he had already cracked the code, mastered reading, and become a successful contributor to society. None of that would have been possible though if it were not for Mr. Emmerich. You see, Jeff came from a home where he in many ways should have joined the statistics. He was an ignored child, left to stumble alone through his learning troubles. Luckily though, like church for me, Mr. Emmerich would not let that happen to Jeff. He was a "community father," who had the character to look beyond his own family and help raise a lost boy named Jeff.

Today, Jeff and I both attend church. We love church. In no uncertain terms, we believe the church is the greatest untapped force for good in the entire world.

Today the "poor in spirit," the "least of these," and "the stranger on the side of the Jericho Road" take many forms, but one of those forms is the one in five adults in the U.S. who never learned to read. Their alarm went unanswered at 10 years old . . . and today they are our poor, our prisoners, our addicts, our sex workers . . . and so many others who we have tossed aside.

A Harvard study found that the most determinative factor to a child succeeding, regardless of class or circumstance, was having one healthy and encouraging adult.[6]

If we, the church, can come together and support these under-resourced children before that alarm goes off at age 10, we may very well be rescuing an entire generation from poverty, prison, prostitution, addiction, and more.

How can that not be the work of the people of God?

So, in so many ways, this book is about *you*. It is about us . . . *all* of us.

Jeff and I want to take you on a journey through these pages. We have made this book easy to consume and full of hopeful encouragement.

You may want to read one short entry each day as part of your daily devotions. You may take it on a weekend holiday and read it straight through. We even made it fairly easy for the busy pastor to skim.

However you consume it, we are thankful that you are going on this journey with us. We believe in you. We believe that your heart wants to love the things that God loves.

And while you are walking through this book, keep in mind:

The simple fact you are able to read these pages is a gift from God . . .
. . . a gift that one in five U.S. adults do not possess.

TeachAKidToRead.com

1
DISRUPTING GENERATIONAL POVERTY

> **Learn to do right; seek justice.**
> **Defend the oppressed.**
> **Take up the cause of the fatherless;**
> **plead the case of the widow.**
> **—Isaiah 1:17**

The Campaign for Grade-Level Reading is a grassroots-to-govenors network promoting grade-level reading . . . they are truly one of the smartest, most effective, and most activated groups in the U.S. Our friend Ron Fairchild, a senior consultant with this group, says this:

> **The Campaign's starting point is really about *disrupting generational poverty.***

And the earliest and one of the best predictors we have for whether and to what extent kids are going to succeed in school and life is third-grade reading proficiency.[7]

Through the process of writing this book, we considered titling it *Disrupting Poverty*. We discussed, even argued, regarding that title because it embodies something vitally important: the connection between *illiteracy* and *poverty*.

In the pages that follow you will get a chance to see the importance of literacy from 50 different angles. You are going to learn about the connection between literacy and your pocketbook. You will learn about the role of literacy in the U.S. story and in modern society. You will learn about how struggling school children are the *best* opportunity for God's people to be with the "least of these," just as Jesus commanded us to do.

Ultimately, we must see early childhood literacy as a *justice* issue.

When we say, "disrupting generational poverty," we are referring to several vitally important ideas.

One is that injustice, oppression, and poverty—without intervention—quickly become generational. The pain, lack of opportunity, and limitations are passed from parents to children. We believe this is why the LORD instructed Moses to include mechanisms like the *Year of Jubilee* into the Torah Law to forgive all debts and redistribute opportunity (Leviticus 25).

In Luke's Gospel, Jesus echoes the Jubilee spirit when he began his ministry with the words:

> The Spirit of the Lord is on me,
> because he has anointed me
> to proclaim good news to the poor
> He has sent me to proclaim freedom for the prisoners
> and recovery of sight for the blind,
> to set the oppressed free,
> to proclaim the year of the Lord's favor.
>
> —Luke 4:18-19

Two, justice always requires disruption. It necessitates benevolent and courageous action. This is why Jesus was, daily, willing to shake up society by touching, valuing, and elevating the forgotten, marginalized, isolated, and rejected. In Mark's Gospel, chapter 1, Jesus begins his ministry by compassionately visiting, touching, affirming, and bringing healing to a leper (and many others).

Three, disrupting poverty is not about deifying wealth, it is about equity, opportunity, and esteem. This is why Jesus equated the Gospel of the Kingdom with feeding, clothing, and "inviting in" (Matthew 25:35-36). It is why Isaiah quotes the LORD with these words:

> See, I will create new heavens and a new earth . . .
> They will build houses and dwell in them;
> they will plant vineyards and eat their fruit.

No longer will they build houses and others live in them, or plant and others eat.
—Isaiah 65:17, 21-22

The question is, do the people of God want to practice the "new heavens/new earth" now? In the twenty-first century, Isaiah's vision of opportunity and esteem requires closing the education gap. Remember what Ron of the Campaign said:

> **One of the best predictors we have [of a child's success in school and life] is 3rd-grade reading proficiency.**
> **—Ron Fairchild, Campaign for Grade Level Reading**

#DisruptingPoverty

#PreventativeJustice

Ron Fairchild, in his own words:

PART ONE

IT'S FOR THE CHILDREN

FOR AS MUCH AS YOU HAVE DONE
IT TO THE LEAST OF THESE,
YOU HAVE DONE IT UNTO ME.

—JESUS

2
FOR SUCH A TIME AS THIS

**Little ones to Him belong, they are weak
but He is strong...**
—an old children's Sunday school song

This book is concerned for the often-forgotten children of our communities. It is about children who were born with no vote in where they live, what their economic condition might be, and with no ability to choose what sort of support structure they might be afforded.

They are just babies . . . and then toddlers . . . and then young children. Someday, they will have a voice and try to advocate for themselves, but until that day, who will be their advocate? Who will be their voice?

Here are a few statistics to consider. While you read them, ask yourself, "What is going on here?" (Note: most of the statistics in this book are from before the COVID-19 pandemic wherein schools were closed. It will be years before we know how much worse all of these numbers actually are today, however studies are now suggesting the pandemic has put us even further behind.[8])

Each year 1.3 million 4th-graders in the U.S. read below basic levels, according to the National Center for Education Statistics (NCES).[9]

According to a 2023 *Wall Street Journal* article, the Nation's Report Card federal reading test showed that reading scores for 4th-graders dropped from 35% in 2019 to 33% in 2022, as a result of the COVID-19 pandemic.[10]

Students who don't meet proficient reading standards by the end of 3rd grade are four times more likely to drop out of high school without graduating than students who pass the standards.[11]

High school graduation can be reasonably predicted by knowing someone's reading skill at the end of 3rd grade.[12]

What did you notice? Do you see the golden window of opportunity?

You see, the U.S. education system *puts a ticking clock on every child*, and when that child's alarm goes off, for most of them, there is no second chance.

It is as simple as it is tragic. It is a phrase repeated over and over again in the literacy world:

From 1st grade through 3rd grade, children *learn* to *read*, and from 4th grade on, children *read* to *learn*.[13]

After the alarm goes off, there are *very few resources* for learning to read.

In fact, from that day forward, that child's reading proficiency is essential to continuing the education process.

That is why this is the golden window of literacy.

In these pages, we will discuss the numerous destructive outcomes waiting for these young children who, by no fault of their own, never learned how to read. You will read about these outcomes, outcomes the Bible seems to care about and calls us to overcome.

However, it is also necessary for us to understand our context . . . *for such a time as this:*

1. In the world we live in today, *reading is an essential survival skill.* There is almost no way to navigate

life, find purpose, and positively contribute to society without the ability to read.

2. If children, especially children from under-resourced backgrounds, don't learn to read by 3rd grade, *statistically they **never** will.*

3. Currently, we are sentencing *1.3 million 4th-graders to a life they don't deserve.* There are simply not enough healthy adults with the compassion to help close this gap.

Who will go? Who will give those children a chance before their golden window closes? Who will say, "Send me"?

The stakes are high. Watch:

3
THE THING TONY CAMPOLO SAID

For as much as you have done it to the least of these, you have done it unto me.
—Jesus

Many years ago, when I was a young seminarian, I was invited at the last minute to a dinner party with Tony Campolo.

Now, I had known of Dr. Campolo, the famous theologian and activist, since I was a boy. My youth group pastor loved to share with us clips of Campolo on stage—his round face, dramatic eyes, and wet lips passionately appealed to all who would listen, exhorting us to follow Jesus.

And there I was, decades later, suddenly asked to have dinner with the man.

I arrived at the stately dining room. Tony was making the rounds, making sure he shook hands with the two dozen invitees before the meal began, myself included. He asked me my name and for a bit of my story before quickly moving on to the next guest. I looked around the room to see seminary leaders, head pastors, and presidents of mission agencies . . . and the least of the least, me.

When the host called the meal to begin, we each took our assigned seats. I, as was appropriate to my station, was seated at the foot of the table, the farthest chair from Dr. Campolo.

Through each of the courses, the esteemed theologian held court. He was the perfect conversational host. He never allowed the velocity of the conversation to slow. He deftly engaged the varied personalities around the table while leading spirited conversations about the Gospel, God's kingdom, justice, and compassion.

At one particularly poignant moment, toward the meal's climax, Campolo cleared his throat and, with narrowed eyes, scanned every face at the table to make sure he had everyone's unabated attention.

"What is your theology of the poor?!" he bellowed, his eyes moving from face to face.

No one answered.

No one moved.

"I'll ask again," he said and he pleaded, "What is your theology of the poor?"

Again, no response was offered. Undiscouraged, Campolo's eyes turned and locked onto the farthest end of the table. "Young theologian," his voice shooting the length of the 20-foot-long table, "Surely you have an answer for us. What is *your* theology of the poor?"

To my shame, all I could do was stammer: a stream of unrelated seminary words nonsensically strung together.

To his credit, Dr. Campolo, with compassion in both his interruption and his eyes, rescued me from my embarrassment with this declarative . . .

> **Our theology of the poor is simple . . . when you look into the face of the poor, you look into the face of Jesus.**

He took a beat to see if his words had hit their mark and continued, "When you look into the face of the poor, you look into the face of Jesus. Is that not the most direct application of Jesus's words, 'For as much as you have done it to the least of these, you have done it unto me?'"

Though the years have come and gone since that evening in that ornate dining room, I can replay the moment in my museum of memories as if it were just a few days ago.

This week, I stumbled across these words, again by the esteemed Tony Campolo:

> **Jesus never says to the poor: "Come find the church," but he says to those of us in the church: "Go into the world and find the poor, hungry, homeless, imprisoned."**

The command of the good doctor looks true to me ... but when you put Tony's two exhortations together, it seems that we go find the poor, not because we have to, but because it is a gift! We get to find Jesus there.

> **Truly I tell you, whatever you did for one of the least of these brothers and sisters of mine, you did for me.**
> **—Matthew 25:40**

Watch *Least of These* film here:

4
HOW TO BUILD A BRAIN

**Love the LORD your God with
all your mind.**
—Jesus

How do you build a brain?

A baby is born and even though it is so very small, amazingly, that infant's brain is already 25% developed.[14] By 1 year old, the brain is basically half developed and by age 6 that child's brain is about 95% developed.[15] Incredible! From age 6 to 25, the brain basically completes the final 5%.

This explains why—as a 53-year-old—I can still recite the lyrics to every '80s TV sitcom, but half the time I can't remember why I walked into the kitchen.

Those early pliant years of brain development are essential and transformational. It is why children can learn multiple languages almost without trying. It is how my toddler children were able to pretend like they were reading their Dr. Seuss books to me, but in reality their little brains were reciting them flawlessly from memory. An early brain is a truly miraculous thing.

We will mention in this book many times the golden window of learning. Often we talk about it from the school curriculum side: from 1st grade to 3rd-grade children *learn to read*, from 4th grade on they *read to learn*. After 3rd grade there is no more curriculum energy put toward literacy (and often no more opportunity.)

What we haven't stated clearly is this: schools are not cruel! They aren't. Schools and school systems don't stop teaching reading to harm children, they do so because the golden window is also about brain development. Up until age 10 (when the brain is at least 95% developed but still growing) is the optimal time for reading acquisition. And all things being equal, the child's brain is ready to read, like it never will be again.

It is in that phrase, *"All things being equal,"* where we find the tragedy.

How do you build a healthy brain?

HOW TO BUILD A BRAIN

It is not complicated. Like with any building project, it is all about the quality of the materials. To build a healthy brain it takes good, nutritious, vitamin-rich food, a good environment, good relationships, lots of rest, lots of encouragement and praise, constructive play, and lots and lots of words: big words and small words, good words and book words, and words around the dinner table.

And with the right materials, the brain can fully actualize, especially during that golden window.

Now, how *not* to build a brain? Give it bad materials, such as little food or cheap, processed food, an unhealthy environment, less rest, less hugs, unconstructive play, harmful relationships, and of course, less words, bad words, and worst of all, no words.

When you add trauma to this, in all its forms, the brain goes into a state of fight, flight, or freeze, and the construction work on that brain shuts down.

It is no wonder that so many little brains struggle to learn.

Well, the good news is that this is not the whole story. A fancy word called "neuroplasticity" basically means the brain is made to heal itself or spring back . . . as long as we provide the right materials.

By now, you can probably guess what those good materials would be. For this context, the materials that matter most are: positive encouragement, lots of words, and most importantly . . . positive human-to-human connection.

That's right—a healthy, caring human can actually heal a brain and give that child a chance.

Watch *Build a Brain* video here:

5
TRAUMA

In this world you will have hardship, but take heart, I have overcome the world.
—Jesus

When one sits down with education experts, especially those who deal with the many-layered, many-factored dimensions of quality learning, they always seem to include the impact of trauma (or toxic stress).

Trauma originates, according to the Substance Abuse and Mental Health Services Administration (SAMHSA)[16], when a child experiences:

- Psychological, physical, or sexual abuse or assault
- Community or school violence
- Witnessing or experiencing domestic violence
- National disasters or terrorism
- Commercial sexual exploitation

- Sudden or violent loss of a loved one
- Neglect
- Serious accidents or life-threatening illness
- Chronic hunger, cold, or lack of safety

More than two-thirds of children in the U.S. reported at least one traumatic event by age 16, according to the U.S. Department of Health and Human Services.[17] And, according to Harvard, when a child experiences trauma, it cripples their ability to learn.[18]

Ongoing trauma (toxic stress) has a cumulative toll on a child's mental and emotional health. The more adverse events or factors, the greater the likelihood of developmental delays and other problems.

What are developmental delays? Ongoing trauma inhibits the parts of the brain responsible for *reasoning*, *learning*, and *emotion*. These experiences are toxic to their otherwise quickly growing brain, arresting their brain's natural fast and formative growth and instead, effectively paralyzing the brain. It does not just slow growth, *it can diminish it*. This impacts learning, behavior, and emotional and mental health.

Children can often not articulate what they have experienced.

They definitely cannot understand it.

Believe it or not, though, they have come to believe it is "normal."

**For childhood victims of trauma,
learning is stolen.**

Okay. That was a lot. Forgive me.

Maybe take a deep breath. Maybe a few. Seriously . . . in with the good air, out with the bad.

I admit it. I was trying to knock you off balance. I wasn't trying to be mean. Some things are just too serious to sugarcoat.

It is difficult, isn't it, to even imagine, not to mention hold onto, the great avalanche of pain in this world?

It is even more difficult when it happens to folks who probably didn't have a vote or any agency in their pain. And finally, sometimes we need to remember that this stuff is happening in our county, in our town, and in our neighborhood.

So I leave you with a bit of good news that, at this point, will not surprise you.

In Harvard's study[19] called, "The Impact of Early Adversity on Children's Development," the summary stated:

During these sensitive periods, healthy emotional and cognitive development is shaped by *responsive, dependable interaction with adults* . . .

For the skeptics among you, I admit, I cherry-picked that quote. A reading mentor is not a cure-all. Childhood trauma is too significant to treat it that simply.

But in a world where too many children have few to no "responsive, dependable interaction with adults," I think even the skeptics have to agree that . . .

> **When a child spends one hour a week**
> **with someone who says:**
> **"You are smart."**
> **"I am proud of you."**
> **"You have a future."**
> **"You are worthy of my time."**
> **"I am so lucky to have a friend like you."**
> **. . . the positive impact can't be zero. It can't be.**

Watch *Build a Brain* video here:

6
YOGA BOY

When we write a book like this, we want you to know not just the high-minded ideas and hero stories about literacy. We also want you to know the very real, daily experiences that we have as we engage with the struggling children in our own neighborhoods.

Here is a story from my coauthor, Jeff:

> I live in the suburbs outside of Portland. Most consider it a fairly affluent part of the region. Those same people are surprised when I tell them about all the struggling schools that are hidden in some of the forgotten corners of my suburb.
>
> Just like every Tuesday afternoon, I arrived at my little forgotten school that has a Head Start reading program. It is one of the schools where I read. On this day, there was a squirrelly little angel named

Colton. As I walked into the classroom, Colton was pounding a boy named Andy with his closed fist—the fight was over a dinosaur. I won't excuse his behavior, but I have two grown boys, and let's just say, his behavior didn't surprise me.

Colton was having a bad day. Like so many days as a reading mentor, I could scarcely imagine what had fueled his foul mood. I didn't know what sort of home he came from. I didn't even know if his belly was full. All I knew was he was struggling. Specifically, he was running away from the teachers and aides—like a bird trying to get out of a house. He was causing havoc. While others were reading to kids, there was actual screaming happening because of Colton's "mood."

So of course, the very last kiddo who needs a book read to him was . . . Colton. And of course, who do you think got to be Colton's reading buddy? Me!

Still agitated, Colton grunted that he wanted to read but when I tried, Colton rejected every book

I tried to offer him. Nothing but crossed arms, a shaking head, and "no" after "no."

When I got to the last book in the stack, he whispered, "Yes." It was called *Kid's Yoga*. Oh great! Colton and I were going to go to a cozy corner and read about the exciting topic of yoga!

Let me premise this by saying I am not a child psychology genius. For that, you would have to talk to my wife, Liz. All I knew was Colton was my reading buddy. And therefore, I would do anything to support him, regardless of his mood.

So I thought, *We aren't going to read about yoga, we are going to* do *yoga!* Thank you, Lord—because if you saw my body, you would know that this idea of performing yoga did not come from me, but from the Lord.

Blocking out the room's distractions, Colton opened the book and on the first page was the first yoga pose . . . we did it together. Still holding the position, I suggested to Colton that we could do calming breathing patterns I had learned from a breath-prayer exercise. He loved it. We did another pose—he laughed—and another, and another. Fifteen minutes later we had done every pose twice.

Then, Colton and I put on a yoga clinic for the whole class of young children.

After reading time was over, Colton was calm. His agitation had evaporated. He was back at his desk doing the next school project, and behaving like the angel he truly is.

That night I got an email saying Colton was sad I left and that he had drawn a picture for me—which would be waiting for me the next Tuesday when I came to read.

Colton is an often-troubled kid from a background I couldn't begin to imagine . . . and you know what? I get the privilege of being his friend for a whole school year. It was like a miracle and I got to sit in the front row and watch him transform.

Isn't that just like the Lord? I would not have chosen little Colton, nor would I willfully read a book about yoga. And yet, despite my reluctances, I was the one who got blessed.

We hear stories like this from reading mentors all over the country.

Kids are a miracle.

Watch the Head Start film here:

1
FOR I WAS HUNGRY

For I was hungry and you gave me something to eat, I was thirsty and you gave me something to drink...
—Jesus

Kendall is 9 years old. Her teacher is writing on the board and explaining something related to reading. And while the lesson is no doubt valuable, Kendall is staring off into space, trapped inside a *Peanuts* cartoon, wherein her teacher's voice is little more than a "wah-wah-wah," bouncing off the walls and never finding her mind.

Kendall is hungry. When I say hungry, I mean more than she didn't have breakfast. Kendall lives in a state of hunger. She comes from a home where a full stomach is never a guarantee... and when there is food, it is often the sort of processed, high-calorie, low-nutrition food-substitutes her mother can afford. While Kendall's empty stomach makes it all but impossible to concentrate in her classroom, the really scary part is, even if she could focus, her body has not received the basic nutrition necessary to build her brain.

In the U.S. in 2022, 30 million children were eligible for the free and reduced lunch program.[20] In addition to lunch, many of these children also receive a snack before first period and some are even offered extra food on Friday afternoon to help get them through the weekend.

Programs like these are so needed, but still they function as little more than a Band-Aid.

Thirty million! *Almost one in five children in the U.S. live in households without consistent access to adequate food,*[21] and that means they arrive at school without the nourishment to learn.

> If you spend yourself in behalf of the hungry
> and satisfy the needs of the oppressed,
> then your light will rise in the darkness,
> and your night will become like the noonday.
> —Isaiah 58:10

Conditions like hunger are the result of systemic and generational poverty.

Odds are these kids are hungry because their parents were also raised hungry . . . and their grandparents were too.

There are many reasons why it is generational, but one of those reasons is illustrated by Kendall's story. Kendall's mom is trying hard, working as much as she can, but Kendall is being set up to fail.

Kendall is struggling to concentrate and her body is struggling to find enough nutrition to build what should be a big, beautiful 9-year-old brain. Statistically, Kendall, without some help, is going to fail to learn to read, write, and do math.

According to the National Institute for Literacy, *70% of welfare recipients score low in literacy.*[22] Kendall is not only struggling with hunger today, she is destined to struggle her whole life through.

The connection between illiteracy and poverty is impossible to ignore. Without basic cognitive skills like being able to read, it is impossible to navigate society and get a decent job.

Dr. Donna Beegle, an international expert on poverty and an exception to the rule—she escaped generational poverty herself—says . . .

The number one variable for getting out of poverty, for gaining literacy, *is mentoring.*

The best possible way to care for the hungry is to give them the tools so they never have to be hungry again. For Kendall, that school lunch is going to kick in. And it is going to help her to be able to focus. Now, if only someone, like a reading mentor, comes along and cares enough to make her the center of attention and remind her that she is smart . . . she might just have a future and a hope.

#PreventativeJustice

> **. . . for as much as you have done it to the least of these,
> you've done it unto me.
> —Jesus**

Watch Dr. Donna Beegles video on Poverty and Literacy:

8
FOR I WAS A STRANGER

I was a stranger and you invited me in . . .
—Jesus

Have you ever been to another country and felt painfully aware of how different you were from everyone around you? If you are like me, you couldn't help it. It wasn't just your clothes or perhaps your complexion, it was the way you walked, stood, and mannerisms that you couldn't seem to shake even if you wanted to.

Now imagine all those awkward feelings, but instead of traveling from the most powerful country in the world, you are coming from someplace very small . . . in fact, imagine that you *feel* very small. Now imagine you are just a child, 7 or 8 years old, and thrust into a school full of loud American kids, all bouncing off the walls and yelling. Imagine you could not express yourself. Can you feel it ... deep inside you? Can you feel the isolation? The loneliness? The fear?

There is a great tradition in the Bible for loving the stranger. Moses said:

> You shall treat the stranger who sojourns with you as the native among you, and you shall love him/her as yourself, for you were strangers in the land of Egypt: I am the LORD your God.
> —Leviticus 19:34 (ESV)

The author of Hebrews says, "Do not neglect to show hospitality to strangers." When Jesus is asked, "Who is my neighbor?" He tells a story about a man who loved a stranger from another land.

It is a wonderful thing to live in the twenty-first century. We have the opportunity to love the nations of the world and we can do it so often without having to leave our neighborhoods. It is downright amazing that "neighbor" and "foreigner" can now be the same thing since the nations are traveling to our land.

Go ye into all the world ...
—Jesus

We like to say, "there is nothing intimidating about a 9-year-old," even one who came here from a faraway place.

Families who have moved to our neighborhoods, be it temporarily or with the desire to become citizens, most often place their children in public schools. It has been shown that the single most important element to acclimating to another culture is language acquisition. The most essential ingredient for an immigrant to have a future and a hope is learning to read and converse.

The children of the very "strangers" that Jesus includes in Matthew 25 are sitting in classrooms right now, maybe right down the street from your house or your church. These students feel like they don't belong. They may feel like no one cares about them.

Right now, they are doubting anyone will ever walk through that classroom door and say to them, "You are important. You are worth my time. You are welcome here. I want to be your friend and teach you some things about my language and my culture."

We don't focus very much on the "stranger" in the pages of this book, but if you and your community choose to adopt a school as reading mentors, there is a very good chance that at least some of you will get the great privilege of fulfilling Jesus's admonition, "I was a stranger and you invited me in."

And because you have a good heart, transformed by God, you might respond, just like the sheep in Matthew 25, who said, "When Lord, when were you a stranger and we invited you in." To which Jesus will say . . .

. . . for as much as you have done it to the least of these, you've done it unto me.
—Jesus

From the mouths of babes . . .

FOR I WAS NAKED

For I was naked and you clothed me...
—Jesus

I was raised to be ashamed of nakedness. It was a topic that was not discussed in polite company.

And yet, here is Jesus, in classic Jesus form, talking about taboos. He is on a roll talking about the ignored, the rejected, and the forgotten in society and, in the midst of discussing hunger, imprisonment, and immigration, Jesus engages in a topic I was taught to avoid. He actually said the word ... he said, "naked."

So let's attempt to be just as edgy as Jesus, shall we? Question: Why would Jesus include "naked" in his list of forgotten people?

Who were the naked of Jesus's day? Like "hungry" and "sick," I assume Jesus was talking about individuals most people passed every day but tried their hardest to ignore. I certainly know what it is like to have tunnel vision: Just keep your eyes forward. Pretend they aren't there. Don't get tempted. Don't get distracted.

It is as if Jesus is begging, "Open your eyes. See the people I see." It's a teaching that is as applicable today as it was back then.

So who were the "naked" that Jesus related to so compassionately that he said, "For I was naked . . . when you do it to them, you are doing it to me"?

Was it the extreme poor? Was it the babbling insane? Maybe.

I imagine that Jesus saw naked people every day . . . a class of shameful people the religious pretended weren't there at all.

I'm talking about people in the sex industry. The Bible writers tell multiple stories of Jesus noticing people for whom their naked past had defined them, marginalized them, and literally cast them out of society.

> If a brother or sister is poorly clothed and lacking in daily food,
> and one of you says to them, "Go in peace, be warmed and filled,"
> without giving them the things needed for the body, what good is that?
> So also faith by itself, if it does not have works, is dead.
> —James 2:15-17 (ESV)

Does illiteracy have anything to do with those enslaved by the naked life?

You might already be nodding because the connection is so obvious.

The connection is also far too easy to ignore. While the estimates vary widely, according to one source there are an estimated 40 million victims of human trafficking in the world, most commonly for sexual exploitation or forced labor.[23] If I am being honest, I don't want to think about it. It is easier to just avoid those parts of town and put an internet filter on my laptop.

Jesus, however, didn't ignore the naked . . . so let's consider how illiteracy contributes to young women and men becoming the naked of society:

- Illiterate kids drop out of school and are left with *fewer options* to make a living.

- Illiterate kids have less teaching and awareness about the *impact of the choices* they make. (Note: this is also why illiterate teenage girls are much more likely to get pregnant than literate girls.[24])

- Illiterate kids, after dropping out, are often left without healthy structures and have too much time to fill. *Idle hands . . .*

- Illiterate kids very often come from poverty and are often *asked to financially contribute* from a young age.
- Illiterate kids often *lack support systems* that teach self-esteem and confidence.
- Tossed-aside young people are the *prime targets* for human traffickers.
- Young people who feel like *rejects and failures* might look for *anyone* to love them.

Illiteracy is a prolific engine of the sex industry and sex-related destructive choices (like unwanted pregnancy).

It is difficult for a typical guy like me to imagine how I could rescue someone out of their naked life. I wouldn't know where to start. However, I can imagine how I might keep someone from the naked path all together. I can imagine how I could become a reading mentor and tell a young soul that they are valuable, that they are smart, and that they have a future and a hope.

On a wide range of issues, if only we could move upstream, go back in time so to speak, before tragedy befalls the young.

Children are not born as sex workers or as the sex-destroyed . . . they are abducted onto the naked path by poor choices and by very real predators . . . and are therefore forever scarred. If only someone had come along and shown them a different path.

#PreventativeJustice

> ... **for as much as you have done it to the least of these, you've done it unto me.**
> **—Jesus**

10
FOR I WAS SICK

I was sick and you visited me . . .
—Jesus

Jason has always been stumbling to catch up. Like so many students, even though he was far below educational benchmarks, every year Jason was "failed up" to the next grade level. He was happy to not have to endure the embarrassment of repeating grades . . . but every year he would enter class more lost, more confused, more alone, and feeling more and more like a failure. Jason did what too many kids in his situation do—he decided to avoid the pain.

Avoiding the pain started with missing more and more days of school.

Now, with more time than he knows what to do with and more shame and failure than he knows how to get rid of, what do you think Jason eventually does? He decides to make the pain go away, and for a kid destined for failure, the easiest way to do that is to get high.

Like too many kids who grow up in the streets, Jason knows there is always a way to stop feeling . . . a way to get numb . . . and that's to get high.

Illiteracy, education struggles, and drug use have been linked in numerous studies. It is ironic that the last people who can afford to infuse mood-altering substances into their half-developed brains are kids who are already struggling to keep up. It is a vicious cycle. The experience of failure leads to substance use and substance use keeps kids from going back to school, and the spiral goes deeper and deeper.

Jesus seemed very concerned for the sick. He noticed the infirm along the road when seemingly no one else did. He traveled considerable distances to visit the ill. He risked public ridicule to tend to those in emotional and physical pain.

> If anyone has the world's goods and sees his brother in need, yet closes his heart against him,
> how does God's love abide in him?
> Little children, let us not love in word or talk but in deed and in truth.
> —1 John 3:17-18 (ESV)

Kids who don't learn to read by 4th grade are twice as likely to end up abusing substances as teenagers (or even younger). While it cannot be the only factor, there does seem to be a connection between those early experiences of failure and the need to numb out.

Every recovering addict I know wishes they could go back to their younger selves and convince them to never start using in the first place.

As a reading mentor, you might just be providing—not just the sense of success that comes with reading—but also the self-esteem and self-worth a child receives just from sitting once a week with a committed adult.

The best way to help the sick may be to help make sure they never get sick in the first place.

This piece started with a discussion of addiction, an abuse against the body/soul/mind that we often associate with young people—however illiteracy is associated with far more medical problems than just substance abuse.

There are too many to name them all, but I will leave you with this: illiteracy is associated with a 75% increased risk of dying earlier as well as an increased risk of living with health issues.

It is staggering the number of ways that helping a child to read could potentially impact their life for good.

#PreventativeJustice

> **... for as much as you have done it to the least of these, you've done it unto me.**
> **—Jesus**

The importance of literacy from Forth Worth, TX:

11

FOR I WAS IN PRISON

For I was in prison and you visited me . . .

—Jesus

Curtis was raised in poverty, occasionally homeless, even though his mother did all she could just to keep her son fed. He couldn't read. He dropped out of school young and was arrested at 17 for behaviors he only learned because he believed he had no other options. In prison, he would hustle every morning to get the sports section of the newspaper and take it back to his cellmate, who would read it to him.

Curtis' story is not unique.

According to the *Chicago Tribune*, 60% of young men entering prison cannot read above a 3rd-grade level.[25]

Correctional Education Association reports that 75% of inmates read at low to very low levels.[26] In the same report, we can read that 85% of juveniles who interact with the criminal court system read at low or very low levels.

There is a popular story told among education activists that there is a state where the government plans how many prison beds to add over the next 10 years by counting how many 4th grade boys are unable to read. There are some who swear this story is true. Others say it is a parable, created to illustrate just how dire the connection is between illiteracy and incarceration, especially for young boys. Real or parable, this story hurts the heart.

Like most systems that destroy lives, the ingredients that cause a person to go to prison are diverse, layered, disparate, and vary from person to person and community to community. That being said, it is impossible to ignore the correlation between illiteracy and incarceration.

One point two million kids drop out of school every year[27] and the vast majority of those are not meeting basic education standards. What are these 1.2 million kids to do? If they can't read, they can't get a driver's license. If they can't read, they can't fill out a job application. If they can't read, they won't even be able to apply for public services without assistance.

What are they to do?

Children are not born criminals.

In 2021, *1.2 million* people were imprisoned, according to the *Sentencing Project*.[28] Where have we seen that number before? Look back two paragraphs.

> I, the LORD, have called you in righteousness;
> I will take hold of your hand . . .
> to free captives from prison
> and to release from the dungeon
> those who sit in darkness.
> —Isaiah 42:6-7

Our friend, Marquise, taught us that in 1855, the American abolitionist and statesman Frederick Douglass said,

**It is easier to build strong children
than fix broken men.**

Marquise was very much like Curtis, the story from the beginning of this chapter. He also was born in tough circumstances. He also failed at school. He also got into criminal behavior. He also was imprisoned as a young person and was unable to read. In time, Marquise got out. He got out partially because he learned to read. He knows he was the exception, one of the lucky ones.

Today, Marquise dedicates himself to being a reading mentor to little boys, boys that to him are just like looking in the mirror. He wants a better future for them. He doesn't want them to experience all the pain and shame and suffering that he endured. He lives by the words of Douglas: *"It is easier to build strong children than fix broken men."*

You see, Marquise knows the best way to bless prisoners, like Jesus said, is to *make sure they never end up incarcerated in the first place.*

#PreventativeJustice

> **. . . for as much as you have done it to the least of these, you've done it unto me.**
> **—Jesus**

Watch Marquise's and Rico's story here:

12
NAS AND CRAIG

> **O Lord, you hear the desire of the afflicted;
> you will strengthen their heart; *you will
> incline your ear to do justice to the fatherless
> and the oppressed.***
> **—Psalm 10:17-18 (ESV)**

Craig is a middle-class man living in a midsized U.S. city. He works in construction and, by his own admission, does not have the most dynamic personality. He wanted to get involved in mentoring, specifically in the area of reading.

His church worked with a local literacy program and Craig went to one of the volunteer gatherings. What did he see? A room full of big, gregarious personalities, the kind of folks who were probably once summer camp counselors. They would break into song or laughter at a moment's notice. If this is what being a reading mentor looked like, Craig feared he didn't fit the bill.

Nas was raised by his grandmother along with his two younger siblings. The elderly woman's life was hard, but she always made sure the children were cared for as best as she could manage.

There are about three million children in the U.S. today who are being raised by grandparents: some because the parents aren't able to care for their child, some because the parents just don't want to, and some because the parents are gone.

When Nas was 8 years old, his grandmother died.

Nas' mother was located and the three siblings were returned to her care. Nas had to move. He had to change schools. He had to change his whole world.

One day, a caregiver in a children's organization came to find Nas at his home. It took some looking. She found him in a lean-to structure, roughly attached to the back of a multistory building in a low-income neighborhood. The lean-to was maybe 15 feet wide. No windows. No kitchen. Nas slept on the floor.

Nas had a difficult time adjusting to a mother he did not know and a place that didn't feel like home.

When Craig looked in the mirror he saw a gruff man. He tried to imagine himself as a joke-telling, affable person. He couldn't.

We are empathetic to Craig's feelings, but at the same time, we find them baffling.

As we travel the country, we meet so many good people who are somehow convinced they don't have the personality or skillset of an effective reading mentor. Most of these people don't understand. There are no personality rules. There is no archetype. There is no ideal. Remember, even the stodgiest of old men's hearts can melt at the sight of a grandchild.

Craig overcame his doubts and volunteered anyway . . .

Of course, Craig was paired with Nas.

At that point, Nas' emotional struggles were affecting everything. He had never been great at school, but now his performance was taking a nosedive. No one knew what to do. His teachers didn't know what to do. And certainly, Craig didn't know what to do.

So Craig did the only thing he knew how to do. He treated Nas like a young man. He taught him how to shake hands. He taught him how to fist bump, sit up straight, and look an adult in the eyes when he talked. And they spent untold hours working on Nas' reading. *You have to read to survive as a man in this world.*

It is hard to explain the way a stranger is able to enter a child's life and become a formative figure. Of course, no one can replace a parent, but still, the impact can be profound.

Believe it or not, Nas caught up. Craig completed his six-month mentor commitment . . . but it didn't end there.

Craig and Nas stayed connected all the way through elementary school and into high school. Craig was there for Nas . . . and I guess you could say that Nas was there for gruff Craig.

Today, Nas has graduated high school.

He is enrolled at community college.

He attends Craig's church.

He works at a local restaurant and helps support his mom and two siblings.

Craig would say, "My friend Nas, he is a man, a wonderful man."

The power of mentors from Vancouver, Washington:

13
KNIT TOGETHER

> **For You created my inmost being; You knit me together in my mother's womb.**
> **—King David**

We want to be very careful with this topic. Please be patient with us as we try to express the heart of so many of our friends who care very deeply about their faith and about childhood literacy. We are very aware that this subject has complicated implications, and still, we feel it is important to delicately address it.

Illiteracy is unfortunately about unwanted pregnancies. It is about unborn babies. It is about teenage mothers. It is about babies who end up as orphans and in foster care.

Young girls suffer illiteracy at about the same rate as young boys.

The biggest factor in a young child's academic success is their mother's reading skill, according to the National Institutes of Health. This means that when an illiterate girl gets pregnant, it is statistically very likely that her child(ren) will not read either.

There is nothing that illustrates the generational impact of illiteracy (and other correlated issues) than teen pregnancy.

When a girl doesn't excel in reading (and in school generally) one of her destinations is early pregnancy.

The University of Pennsylvania did a study and discovered that girls who struggle in reading are two and a half times more likely to give birth in their teens than girls with even average reading skills. Even more starkly, the American Public Health Association found that girls who struggle in reading are two and a half times more likely to give birth in their *early* teens. While these statistics are overwhelming and represent untold numbers of unwanted babies born into a life of poverty, marginalization, cognitive struggles, and dependence on public assistance, that is not even the whole story . . .

These studies are only about babies brought to term.

What about the countless pregnancies that never make it to birth? What about the untold numbers of those underdeveloped wombs that are unable to carry a baby to term? One thing I think most of us can agree upon, is that we want to protect little girls from unwanted pregnancies.

Yes, births among teens are shockingly higher among girls who struggle in reading, this we know, but when you add to that the number of miscarried pregnancies . . . the impact is beyond comprehension: impact in numbers of lives affected . . . impact on emotions and mental health . . . impact on economics and opportunity. The list goes on and on.

I wish there was an inspirational ending to this short chapter. Even as I write it, I feel the sadness. As with so many of these discussions, reading and education is not a cure-all. However, it has been shown to greatly contribute to better choices, higher self-esteem, and increased hope and opportunity for the future.

Pregnancy is a gift from God. It is one of the great opportunities to co-create with the Divine. It was given to us as a point of celebration and gratitude. So, it is particularly tragic when something so beautiful is regarded as a "regret," a "burden," or a "mistake."

Become a reading mentor and you may be the voice of affirmation and opportunity that redirects a young person away from teenage pregnancy.

Teach a girl to read, give a girl a chance.

#PreventativeJustice

14
"TYPICAL" MEETS "NORMAL"

The reading mentor all but shook with excitement as she pulled open the heavy industrial door, walked beneath the hydraulic-hinged metal arm, and entered the cathedral of learning called "public elementary school."

This woman is wonderfully typical in every way: typically dressed, typical speech, typical height . . . by all accounts from the most typical of backgrounds imaginable.

But on this day, if you were to ask her how she is feeling, I am sure she would declare that the next hour of her life is anything but typical. In fact, for her, it is exceptional. It may be the best hour of her week. Why? Because she is about to meet with her four-foot-tall reading buddy.

The two talk over each other as each explains how happy they are to be at their "reading hour." The reading mentor knows that they need to get around to reading, but first she wants to get caught up on all her reading buddy's news: her teacher, her classroom, the playground, and especially her cat.

Satisfied they are sufficiently caught up, the mentor slides a book in front of her little buddy and carefully opens to the first page. The child's chin rests on the library table's surface as her eyes dance across the pages. Her mentor is overwhelmed by how normal her mentee seems . . . her hair pulled behind her ears . . . her backpack pinned between her body and the chair's vertical back because, in her excitement, she never thought to take it off.

The girl carefully reads, emphasizing each sound aloud:

"I loo-ooked do-own at the pay-paper on my de-SK."

How could I be so lucky, thought this "typical" mentor, who simply volunteers one lunch hour a week to read with this lovely "normal" girl.

It will not surprise you to know that this little girl is anything but "normal" . . . at least not like the old TV show *Brady Bunch* normal. Her reality is very different.

Her principal told us in his deep baritone voice, "There is a lot of stress that our children bring to school before they get here. I can't imagine what half of them go through. We are fighting against neighborhoods. We are fighting against parents that are not focused on their children."

Her dedicated teachers confess to us about their daily experiences with their children: "Some may be hungry. Some may be homeless. Some may be from broken homes. Their electricity has been turned off. They are foster children. We have children that are raising entire families by themselves. Mommy and Daddy are not at home. They don't have books at home. They wouldn't get books read to them."

These teachers we met with could not contain the sadness they felt for the many children who need more than they can offer. They say, "I am only one person. I have dozens of children pulling at me every moment of the day."

One teacher, with skin the color of coffee ice cream, exhaled, "If these kids had just *a little more help.*"

This "typical" reading mentor cannot possibly know what her little reading buddy brings to school each day. Her backpack is full of more than papers and pencils; she also brings chaos, clutter, and confusion.

The mentor also needs to know that is she is anything but "typical." To this seemingly "normal" little girl, she is far more. She is exceptional. She is a ray of light in her otherwise often dark world.

And, through their time together, this little girl is being given a real chance.

15
SELF-ESTEEM

When I was a boy, like so many young people, I had an almost impossible time seeing myself as anything more than a failure. Even though I came from a middle-class family and a two-parent home, self-esteem was still elusive.

I was smaller than all my classmates. I was awkward. I stumbled over my own feet on the ball field and I said the wrong things at all the wrong times in class. Each year I was demoted into the rudimentary reading and math classes. I am not complaining—I am trying to set the stage.

At a particularly tender stage in my development, a man named Jerry walked into my life. He was not a teacher. He was not a relative. He was simply a man of faith who, for reasons that confused my half-developed mind, decided I was important. He chose to spend time with a "failure" like me.

It wasn't his job to spend time with me. He didn't know my family. In fact, you would be hard-pressed to find any connection between Jerry and that awkward boy named Tony. And yet, he prioritized a clumsy, small, and "rudimentary" boy.

Jerry told me:

"You are significant."

"You have a future that is greater than you can imagine."

Again, I was a kid from relative privilege, and yet now, decades later, I still cherish my memories of Jerry. They live warm in my heart.

Now imagine the impact a "Jerry" would have on a child from an under-privileged or under-resourced background, a small human who may not have many, if any, supportive and stable adults in their life. Imagine how impactful those same words of *significance* and *a great future* might be.

The Harvard University's Center for the Developing Child has done extensive research about what factors affect mental/academic/emotional health in children. In conclusion to much of that research, Harvard published this conclusion:[29]

SELF-ESTEEM

Science shows that *children who do well despite serious hardship* have had at least *one stable and committed relationship with a supportive adult*. These relationships buffer children from developmental disruption and help them develop "resilience," or the set of skills needed to respond to adversity and thrive.

Let those words from one of the world's great academic research institutions sink in.

There are disclaimers. Certainly, the Harvard study is talking about the many-layered impact of stable and supportive adults that cannot be fully embodied in a reading-mentor relationship. Yes, illiteracy is just one component of a child's woe-filled future. And yet, the conclusion of Harvard's study remains clear, even remarkable.

Are you "a supportive adult" who can offer "one stable and committed relationship" for one academic year to help a child do well?

One of the things we hear over and over and over again from literacy experts all across the country, in big cities and small towns, is that the social-emotional impact on a child who has a committed reading mentor is as great, if not greater, than the literacy impact.

Social-emotional impact! That is what literacy experts are proclaiming. And that is what a supportive adult, like *you*, could offer. That is what the Harvard studies are confirming.

> The first baby that I had was very shy, but when she started learning to read and the lightbulb came on, I will never forget the day, that I left there and I was shouting "Lord, thank you!" And the next year when I saw her, her whole demeanor had changed. Her self-esteem was through the roof!
> —Wanda McKinney, Fort Worth reading mentor

The impact of mentors from Texas:

16
THE LEAST OF THESE, THE READING-MENTOR EDITION

Come, you who are blessed of My Father,
inherit the Kingdom prepared for you
from the foundation of the world.

For I would have been ever-hungry and ever-thirsty
but you helped make sure I didn't need to be;

For I was a stranger in this land,
destined to be tossed aside
but when I was still young, you showed me I was wanted;

For I would have been defined by my nakedness
and used for sex
but that never happened, because you told me I was valuable;

For my path was heading for addiction,

disease and early death

but as a child you visited me and gave me some

tools to support a healthy life;

For I was destined for prison, a "statistic" like

too many of my friends

but you showed me I was smart and I could be

somebody without crime.

Truly I say to you

to the extent that you helped prevent

one of the least of these from a crippling path,

you did it unto Me.

Watch the *Least of These* film here:

PART TWO

IT'S FOR THE PEOPLE OF GOD

THE WORD BECAME
FLESH AND BLOOD,
AND MOVED INTO THE
NEIGHBORHOOD.

—JOHN 1:14 (THE MESSAGE)

17
ROSIE

> "I am working two jobs and going to school. You have no idea what it means when you come in and take time to read with my kid."
> —Mom of a Book Club child

Erica is intimidating . . . at least that is what people who know her say about her.

She is statuesque, the daughter of Korean immigrants, and she carries herself with impeccable dignity and elegance. Rarely smiling, she always dresses in a business suit and high heels, and thus towers over her surroundings both physically and psychologically.

Erica was raised in the church, always devout. As a young woman she had volunteered for Christian work both domestically and abroad. With age, her world changed. These days, she has many more responsibilities and requirements. No more running off to the other side of the world. Her idea of being on mission has had to change.

Erica was invited to be a reading mentor alongside her church. Open to the idea, she sat down for five minutes with her executive assistant and they determined together to reserve one lunch hour a week so Erica would be free to meet with a child at a school that was just a short drive from her office.

Rosie is an at-risk child. She struggles with a negative self-outlook and dark thoughts. It affects her schooling. It affects everything.

Rosie's mom only speaks Spanish. She cannot afford to provide therapy or other sorts of assistance to Rosie. She can only afford to give Rosie the remnants of her time. She can do almost nothing to help Rosie with schooling, especially reading in English.

When Erica meets Rosie, Rosie is in 3rd grade.

Before they meet, the volunteer coordinator tells Erica a little about Rosie. She is only reading at a 1st-grade level. The volunteer assures Erica that Rosie is a lovely child but she can be withdrawn. She doesn't engage much with the other children or teachers. She is always quiet . . . sad.

Erica listens. Her face never changes. She nods, stands, and straightens her skirt. She can't help but wonder, *What have I gotten myself into?*

Rosie and Erica start with reading.

Erica does everything by the book. She doesn't try to "spice it up" with banter or jokes. She is there to read and reading is exactly what they do. And at the end of that first session, Rosie, wide-eyed, grabs her hand and pleads, "Are you coming back?"

Week by week, book by book, Erica returns. Rosie's abilities creep up and within months she is meeting each reading benchmark, much to the surprise and delight of her teachers.

"Now I need help in math!" Rosie insists, beginning to advocate for herself in class. She wants to continue to experience success. She loves feeling smart.

I asked Rosie's teacher about her remarkable turnaround, and this is what her teacher said:

I asked Rosie the same thing and she told me, "Ms. Erica believes in me."

Erica still talks about how the experience surprised her. She wasn't so much surprised that Rosie improved—anybody could see there was an exceptional child inside of her wanting to get out. Erica was surprised because she thought she was going to that school to help someone else, and along the way she found herself loving this little girl. Erica believes she was changed most by the relationship.

We get so insulated in our Christian bubble that we never really walk with anyone who is different.

As for Rosie, today she is in middle school and still doing well. She is still advocating for herself and moving well through her classes.

She says she wants to be a therapist when she grows up so she can help other people too.

**The exercise of justice is joy for the righteous
—Proverbs 21:15 (NASB)**

Watch *Piper and Mrs. Martin:*

18
LOVING YOUR NEIGHBOR

**Love the LORD your God . . . and the
second is like it:
"Love your neighbor as yourself."
—Jesus**

The Bible's Red Letters (words of Jesus) are full of many challenging exhortations: "you can move a mountain," "you will handle snakes," "you can forgive sins," "if someone asks for your shirt, give them your coat also."

As a boy in church, I was steered away from the vast majority of these difficult sections. When we did deal with these passages, they were often relegated to theory or diluted into a life principle or dismissed as "a concept for another time or place." To put it simply, they were usually made impractical and irrelevant.

Then there are other challenging teachings that don't seem to be abstract in any way.

They are impossible to ignore because of their clarity and their regular appearance in those pesky Red Letters.

- Blessed are you who are hungry, for you will be filled.
- Bring good news to the poor and proclaim release to the prisoners.
- Love your neighbor as yourself.
- Go, sell all you have and give it to the poor.
- When you have a banquet, invite the poor.
- Woe to you who neglect justice and the love of God.
- As much as you have done it to the least of these (the hungry, thirsty, stranger, naked, sick, prisoner), you have done it to me.
- Be like the Good Samaritan who loved a discarded and hurting foreigner.

Some will debate about the nuances of these passages (and the 2,100 other Bible passages that discuss the poor and discarded), but that might miss the point.

Despite the nuances, it is my experience that *every Christian wants to live so as to reflect the Red Letters more and more.*

LOVING YOUR NEIGHBOR

Every Sunday morning, millions of Americans are reminded that their life is not their own and they exist to love God and love their "neighbor." In the parable of the Good Samaritan, Jesus illustrates the neighbor as someone who might be very different, might come from another class or culture, and might need help but has been ignored.

My experience is that every Christian wants to love as Jesus illustrates, but sometimes they don't know where to start.

Where do we go?

Prisons? *Let's face it, prisons are really scary.*

Soup kitchens? *That sounds intimidating.*

Immigration centers? *I don't know if there are any around here. And I wouldn't have anything to say.*

The Projects? *I have seen the movies.*

Most people don't realize that the "poor in spirit," "the least of these," and "the stranger along the road" can be easily encountered in every neighborhood. Where?

They are in our schools.

They are children.

Many of them are struggling and need a *true* neighbor to assist them. And just a little assistance can go a long way.

If you are 14 to 95 and can read, then you can put Jesus's exhortations into practice in an under-resourced school. You can volunteer today. Don't forget . . .

There is nothing intimidating about a 9-year-old.

19
STORYTELLER

> **All Jesus did was tell stories—a long**
> **storytelling afternoon.**
> **His storytelling fulfilled the prophecy:**
> **I will open my mouth and tell stories;**
> **I will bring out into the open things hidden**
> **since the world's first day.**
> **—Matthew 13:34-35 (The Message)**

Since the dawn of time, humans have told stories. We told stories around the fire at night. We told stories on the front porch. We whisper the last lines of stories so as not to wake the young soul who is drifting off to dreamland.

From the time of their first words, children learn the phrase, "Read to me" (at least we hope they do). And soon after, when the last page is turned, they learn to say, "Again, again, again."

It is like hypnosis. Words like, "Once upon a time . . ." or, "Did I ever tell you about the time . . ." or "There once was a . . ." place humans in a naturally receptive state. From our youngest days, we have been trained to listen to stories. It is like our natural desire to argue or pontificate submits to the soothing tale.

This is why the Bible starts with "In the beginning . . ." It is why Jesus often started with, "There once was a man with two sons . . ." or "Have you considered the lilies of the field . . ."

My sons are not Bible scholars, but if you asked them what makes the Old Testament and the New Testament similar, they would tell you, "Both the Old and New Testaments start with the story parts. The teaching and prophesy parts come later."

Why is that?

If I could be so presumptuous, allow me to offer this small piece of eternal truth:

Stories are the language of the heart.
Arguments are the language of the head.
The job of the head is to justify the
decisions the heart has already made.
This is why the Bible starts with stories.

This is why Jesus led with stories. Have you ever noticed that Jesus often saves his lesson-times for when he is hanging out alone with the disciples, but when he is out in the neighborhoods, he most often leads with stories (we have about 40 of them—I wonder how many more he told)?

If you (and your faith-community) are lucky enough to adopt a school and serve as reading mentors, you will get to practice every week one of the great human skills:

Storytelling

And as you become a better and better storyteller . . .

You will be a better parent/grandparent.
You will be more influential in your company boardroom.
You will be more fun at picnics and parties.

And you will be much better at talking with your friends and neighbors about your faith.

Enjoy a story:

20
A PARABLE

The teacher was walking along a road and turned to his faithful followers and said . . .

Imagine a world where three things are true. First, the land is full of hungry children. Their eyes are bright but fading, their spirits are sad, and their bellies are longing for bread. Second, all around the land, there are factories full of bread-making machinery. The machines are new, bright, and shiny. They are well oiled and fine-tuned. Their engines are warm and their ovens are hot. The only thing these factories lack is grain. Third, separate from the factories but tragically close by are silos full of grain. There is so much grain that the silos overflow. The excess grain is daily carted away and dumped in a landfill.

There is no malice between the three realities in this story. These three realities exist in parallel. The only evil is that these three elements never talk to each other. In fact, it never occurs to them to talk to each other. The children don't know how to ask for bread. The factories just assume grain will come from somewhere, but don't realize the silos are overflowing. And the silos think their purpose is to be filled to overflowing, never considering their "overflowing" is the solution to a tragic problem.

The teacher then said, "This land is a sort of hell. It is a hell on earth."

I am sure this parable has many applications to societal systems that simply don't talk to each other. Why don't these systems talk to each other? There are many reasons. Sometimes it is because of a lack of imagination and creativity. Sometimes it is because of a suspicion or a prejudice. Sometimes it is simple ignorance, the by-product of one system never caring enough to get to know another system, like the factories and the silos in this parable.

It is tempting to focus on the children as the tragedy in this story. However, all three characters in the story are in pain, they are all unfilled, unfulfilled, and unsatisfied.

Yes, the children are tragically hungry. But the factories are also not able to do the very thing they were funded, built, and maintained to do. And the silos don't even realize they are burying when they could be blessing.

In the U.S., this parable is tragically true in the realm of literacy.

Every city is full of kids, many in Title One schools or from under-resourced neighborhoods, who are not learning to read. The clock is ticking on these kids and like the children in the parable with empty stomachs, these kids have empty minds, minds waiting to be filled with the gift of reading before the alarm goes off and the opportunity to read is gone forever.

Almost every city has literacy nonprofits. These are reading factories that are often very well funded, approved by the local government, and enjoy an excellent relationship with the local schools. They know exactly where the greatest needs for reading help exist. They are well-oiled to onboard reading mentors and to train/place caring volunteers in the best situations. Unfortunately, most of these nonprofits run at 10% capacity. They advertise and network, but try as they might, they cannot find enough volunteers who will give just one hour a week, to meet even a fraction of the demand.

And finally, *in every single neighborhood*, there are "compassion-silos" called churches. These churches are overflowing with neighborliness, full of people who are inspired every week to love like Jesus loved, to befriend the neighbor and the stranger, and to be a healing force in the world.

Why don't these groups talk to one another? There are probably many reasons. Many nonprofits and schools don't know if they can trust churches. Many churches don't realize the need or want to do "their own thing." Whatever the excuses, it is tragic . . . all these systems continue unfulfilled . . .

> **. . . and as a result, the children are suffering in a sort of hell on earth.**

21
RETHINKING THE GOOD SAMARITAN

> **Teacher . . . what must I do
> to inherit eternal life?**
> **—Luke 10:25**

I love that Jesus told stories . . . maybe that is why children seemed to like him so much.

Possibly Jesus's most famous story came at an unexpected moment. Often, when Jesus told a story, it just appeared out of his context, as if Jesus was walking down a road and saw a bird and spontaneously opined, "The Kingdom of Heaven is like a sparrow . . ." but not this time. This time Jesus was asked a very specific question, a question that sprouted that day's story.

The question was, "Who is my neighbor?"

It began something like this: Once upon a time (my words) a man was walking from Jerusalem to

Jericho . . . (A marvelous beginning to a story, no wonder it became one of his greatest hits.)

Since I was a boy in Sunday school, I have been told the story of the Good Samaritan. I have been told it hundreds of times. I can even remember performing a version of the story in a play at Bible camp, and in our version the man wounded on the road was an Oregonian (my state) and the Samaritan was a Californian (because we couldn't think of a more unlikeable person than someone from California. You have to forgive us . . . we were only 9 years old).

In all those lessons about the Good Samaritan, I was always told that it was an extraordinary story, on an extraordinary day, about a man who overcame unprecedented odds to sacrificially love another person . . . not just a person, but his enemy. *And* that this act of extraordinary love came at extraordinary cost . . . This is the way it was told. It was so high and lofty that it set a bar I could hardly hope to reach.

But what if we read the story another way?

What if it wasn't an extraordinary day? What if it was just a Tuesday?

What if the Samaritan wasn't helping his *enemy*; what if he was just assisting someone in need, someone who just happened to be different?

Now ask yourself—*how extraordinary were his actions after all?* He didn't fight off the robbers. He didn't try to fix the broken systems that left this man abandoned and alone. He didn't leap tall buildings in a single bound. None of that.

Instead, he was just walking down a road he had probably walked down a hundred times before . . . like it was just an average Tuesday.

He just did the small thing that was right in front of him. He saw a need and said, "Yes."

The stranger needed care. The Samaritan gave him care.

The stranger needed assistance. The Samaritan had a donkey.

The stranger needed healing. The Samaritan had some pocket money.

The Samaritan did the simple thing that he was already equipped to do, with the resources he already carried around every day.

Maybe the story of the Samaritan and the stranger was not so extraordinary after all . . .

In fact, maybe the fact that it was not extraordinary was the most extraordinary thing of all.

And maybe that is why this story is one of Jesus's greatest hits.

What would it look like for you to love your "neighbor" who just happens to be different from you, in a very normal way . . . on a very typical "Tuesday"? Could you find that neighbor in a local school, maybe along a road you have traveled a hundred times before? Could you be the one who stops, offers a little time and resources you already possess?

The one who is faithful in a very little thing is also faithful in much.
—Luke 16:10 (ESV)

22
THE THING C.S. LEWIS WROTE

> "Do not waste time bothering whether you 'love' your neighbor; act as if you did.
> As soon as we do this we find one of the great secrets.
> When you are behaving as if you loved someone, you will presently come to love him."
> —C.S. Lewis from *Joyful Christian*

One of the most beloved and influential thinkers and theologians of the twentieth century was a writer named C.S. Lewis. He is beloved for his vast library of academic books and essays on God and faith, but he may be best known for his stories. It is as if Lewis knew that stories have a power to speak to the heart in a way that teaching struggles to accomplish.

In one book, *The Screwtape Letters*, Lewis tells the story of two demons, discussing the process of distracting and deceiving a single Christian under the younger demon's responsibility.

The older demon, Screwtape, takes great pains to instruct his novice, Wormwood, in the time-tested craft of derailing a Christian's faith. Wormwood is already in trouble for allowing his "patient" (as Screwtape calls him) to become a Christian. Screwtape assures Wormwood that punishment for this failure will soon come. However, Screwtape encourages Wormwood that there is still much work to be done on behalf of "Our Father Below."

One powerful tactic Screwtape teaches is found in his sixth letter to Wormwood. Screwtape writes this:

> Do what you will, there is going to be some benevolence, as well as some malice, in your patient's soul. The great thing is to direct the malice to his immediate neighbors whom he meets every day and to thrust his benevolence out of the remote circumference, to people he does not know. The malice thus becomes wholly real and the benevolence largely imaginary.

The lesson it seems is that benevolence (or loving compassion) is best nurtured when it is experienced in the immediate, in the present, through person-to-person connection. If not, as Screwtape writes, whatever loving compassion the Christian contains will be "largely imaginary."

Lewis seems to be using story to illustrate the command of Jesus:

> "Love the Lord your God with all your heart and with all your soul and with all your mind." This is

the greatest commandment. And the second is like it: *"Love your neighbor as yourself."* All the Law and the Prophets hang on these two commandments.

In response to these commands, Jesus was asked, "And who is my neighbor?" and Jesus responded with a story (great teachers, like children, seem to know the power of stories). The story Jesus told was "The Good Samaritan," a story we have already discussed in earlier chapters, a story showing benevolence to someone nearby, someone who was in great need and yet was being ignored.

It is worth noting that both Jesus and Lewis seem most concerned for the person of faith. It seemed that the showing of benevolence to the person close by was as much, if not more, for the sake and saving of the love-giver as for the love-receiver.

When we love the neighbor in need, we might just be experiencing salvation ourselves.

23
ONE

It would be better that a millstone were hung around his neck and he were thrown into the sea, than that he would cause one of these little ones to stumble.
—Jesus

Jesus speaks of children many times. They seem to have been often on his mind.

In this passage, Jesus brings harsh words to anyone who might harm a child, suggesting that the repercussions of child-harm would be worse than having a large stone tied around the neck (uncomfortable) and then being tossed overboard into the sea (very uncomfortable).

When this passage talks about stumbling, does it mean spiritual deception? Temptation? Physical, psychological, or emotional abuse? Other? All of the above? I'm not sure.

What I would like to focus on though, is a specific word in this short teaching. That word is "One."

Jesus did not say "one of your offspring." He is not saying "one of your nephews or nieces." He is not saying, "one of your Sunday-school kids, Boy Scout troop, children in your suburb, children that look like you, children that 'behave,' children that dress in the way you approve or children that have your same complexion. It simply says, "one of these little ones."

One.

I believe we have a "tribalism" problem.

We come by it honestly, but it is there all the same. We are taught to divide the world up into "tribes" and think, *I am only responsible for my "tribe."*

Unfortunately, our "tribes" are made up of people (and children) that are most often "just like me" . . . they live like me, talk like me, spend like me, dress like me, go to church like me, someday vote like me, look somewhat like me . . . and if they aren't like me, then they must be someone else's responsibility.

However, Jesus says, "one of these little ones." When I read this, I believe that Jesus is asking the disciples to look beyond their "tribes." In similar fashion, Jesus also rebuked his followers when they try to shoo the children away.

Suffice it to say, a decent definition of a Christian is "someone who loves what Jesus loves" and ever since Sunday school I was taught when it comes to children . . . *they are precious in His sight.*

Our schools are full of kids from every background imaginable: poor and rich, loved and discarded, immigrant and native, abundantly supported and those left all alone. The education system is a literal playground of little ones whom Jesus loves.

I would be a fool to suggest that being a reading mentor is a cure-all. I would be a fool to suggest that education specifically is the primary or even secondary application of what Jesus is thinking in these passages.

What I do know is that Jesus wanted his followers to think about how their choices were affecting children, the things they did, and the things they left undone.

In every city there are schools full of little ones who could use just a little bit of extra support.

And while it can seem overwhelming to imagine how to help the hundreds of children, whose futures quite literally hang in the balance *and* who are also within easy driving distance from your house . . .

That is the other great thing about the word "one."

One is a great place to start.

An encouragement from Mother Theresa:

24
I DIDN'T WANT TO DO IT

**And let us not grow weary of doing good,
for in due season we will reap,
if we do not give up.
—Galatians 6:9 (ESV)**

I met Robert on a sunny afternoon while touring Texas. He sat in the pew, his shoulders hunched. He was tall, barrel chested, and silver haired with the countenance of a gruff Morgan Freeman, if that is even possible.

Robert was reluctant to talk. He wasn't mean; he just seemed like a man who didn't consider his particular story worth going on about. His eyes drifted time and again to the stained-glass windows overhead and seemed surprised by each question I asked.

His voice was tired after decades of yelling after teenage boys as they ran up and down the basketball court. He spoke in short sentences about how he was retired now, about how he used to be a high school basketball coach.

I asked him about Jesus, and he stated in his matter-of-fact way, "To be transparent, He loved me first. That's hard to grasp. I struggle. I struggle with arrogance. I'm being honest with you. But His love shows me what a soft heart is. I have to really dig into that."

He seemed bewildered to find himself answering questions about mentoring young children. Over his life he never thought much about little ones.

Robert is not unique. You would never cast him in a film about being a reading mentor. I smiled at the thought of him balancing on one of those little plastic chairs at a short table, fumbling through the little pages of a children's book.

His giant hands were folded in his lap.

I asked him his mentoring story.

The pace of his speech remained steady. *"I really didn't want to do it.* I've been around high school all my life. Elementary school? You're crazy. That's an easy *no*. There was some selfish stuff there, probably. But it was my lack of confidence in myself because I'm not a creative person."

"What changed?"

Robert said, "So, this dear friend of mine named Sweeney, he gouged me every Thursday night at Bible study about being part of a mentoring program. He said to go ahead and go home and pray about it and all that. Well, I didn't pray about that. I didn't. I just . . . I already knew my answer."

I sat silent, waiting for him to continue. He did . . .

"So Sweeney asked me once more. And long story short, I, I went home and I, I just, you know . . . I said, I'll just for Sweeney's sake, alright, I'll give it a shot."

That was a few years ago and Robert is still sticking with it. "To be transparent about it, there are some days I don't want to do it, you know? But when I go up there, I'm always blessed. There's, there's never been a day that I've mentored that I haven't been blessed."

When I ask Robert about his reading buddy, that's when everything changes. Suddenly his voice skips along as he speaks, all the reluctance evaporating. "Christopher was my first child, and I had him for a lengthy time, three years, and we became very close. And he always had a smile on his face and probably didn't want to. There were nine people in his house, two bedrooms. I knew he didn't get much rest, but he would come in with a smile every time."

The stories go on and on until he gets to when Christopher was moving schools and they had to say good-bye.

His eyes become wet as he spoke, "And so we sat in front of the school there and we just cried as we did.

And so he showed me that those three years were totally worth it, totally."

As we are finishing, there is something he keeps saying, like he wants to make sure that I never forget it:

"And the crazy thing about it is, is that the kid's changing you. You're supposed to be mentoring them. But what is ironic and exciting is they're changing you."

He straightens up and confesses, ***"And it changed my life."*** **Then he wipes his eyes on his cuff.**

Watch Robert's story here:

25
A LITTLE ABOUT THE USA

Live an exemplary life in your neighborhood so that your actions will refute their prejudices. Then they'll be won over to God's side and be there to join in the celebration when he arrives.
—1 Peter 2:12 (The Message)

There is a lie. The lie goes something like this: "You can be anything you want to be . . . the American dream is always available." What if that's not true? What if at age 10 your life is already sentenced?

This is the United States of America: over 330 million people live here. Of those 330 million, in round numbers there are 200,000 CEOs,[30] over one million doctors,[31] and 500,000 elected officials[32] running the government. There are 22 million millionaires[33] and 6 million PhDs.[34]

The U.S. has the most Nobel Prize winners, the most Rhodes Scholars, and more than a million international students each year who all had to fight to come here to learn in our institutions of education.

The U.S. has around 98,000 public schools.[35] There are 3.7 million teachers[36] and that's not counting professors, tutors and education aids, counselors, and school administrators. Here, we spend over $795 billion a year[37] on education . . .

AND despite every one of those facts being true . . .

Today . . . 40% of school children cannot read at a basic level.

So, how did we get here?

Here is a little of the story . . .

> When the U.S. was young, education was left to the family and the church. Most people were poor and reading was not required for the vast majority of labor and agrarian jobs.

> Education was for the few, because it was seen as power, so much so that it was illegal to teach a slave to read. Abolitionist Frederick Douglas knew this when he said, "Once you learn to read, you will be forever free."

In time, the U.S. realized it could never become a great nation if it remained an uneducated nation. The U.S. built the greatest system of higher education in human history and set the pace for the coming industrial and technological revolutions. School systems were established in every community and in 1944, President Franklin D. Roosevelt declared education to be *a basic human right*, regardless of race or economic status.

You would think the U.S. had arrived as an educated powerhouse...

But the truth is that literacy peaked in the 1970s. The 1970s!

Over the last 50 years the U.S. has been falling further and further behind much of the rest of the developed world.

Over those same 50 years, the U.S. has helped to map the human genome, touched down on Mars, launched the global internet, and built the most advanced military machine in human history... and yet she can't seem to teach so many of her citizens to read. And with where the economy is headed and with the types of jobs that will be available, the necessity of basic literacy is only increasing. That is a simple fact.

Today, according to the Department of Labor, one in five adults is functionally illiterate[38] . . . and "functionally illiterate" means one in five adults lacks the basic ability to cope with most jobs.

The apostle Peter wrote about being a citizen, "Live an exemplary life in your neighborhood so that your actions will refute their prejudices (The Message)." We are called to do good and care for our neighbors in whatever way our time and place calls us to.

Long, long ago that meant all farmers left a portion of their crops on the ground so that the poor could eat (Leviticus 19), in New Testament times that meant paying taxes to a pagan government (Romans 13).

In our time, one in five of your neighbors can't read.

Learn more about US literacy history here:

26
HEAL SOCIETY

There is a magic window in the life of a child. Up until 3rd grade, children learn to read, after 3rd grade they read to learn. If a child misses the magical window and doesn't learn to read to grade level by 3rd grade, statistically they are sentenced to fall behind for the rest of their lives. Dropping out becomes expected and the American promise of "opportunity" is all but lost.

By now, you know all of the above. It is a huge pillar of the argument to adopt a school or a struggling child by becoming a reading mentor. It is preventative justice. It is impactful compassion. There are, of course, no guarantees that a child who learns to read will not end up in the criminal justice system, chronically on public assistance, or as a worker in the sex industry, but studies indicate that reading can unlock both self-esteem and a sense of hope when that child is still inside that magic window... that fragile season when a whole life is set in motion.

Teach a child to read, give a child a chance.

To be a reading mentor, all you need is a little compassion and the ability to read well enough to model reading to a 9-year-old child. You don't even need to read like an Oxford professor, you only need to be able to put on a smile and read, *"One fish. Two fish. Red fish. Blue fish."*

As a reading mentor, for one hour a week during one school year, there is a real chance you could change the life of a child. And that would be amazing! *But the impact could be **far more** than you even imagine.*

Consider:

- Do you want to help *a child* on the path to becoming a healthy adult? Help them read by 3rd grade.

- Do you want to help overwhelmed *parents* who may be working multiple jobs and are unable to support educational outcomes? Help their children read by 3rd grade.

- Do you want to bless *grandparents* and break the cycles of generational poverty? Help their grandchildren read by 3rd grade.

- Do you want to assist an overtaxed *teacher*, saddled with too large a classroom and too many struggling kids? Give a little help to ease their burden.

- Do you want to help a *school* get the resources they need to help all their children? Help one child meet the benchmarks that school budgets rely upon.

- Do you want to change a *neighborhood* for the next generation and thus change a nation? Help their children read by 3rd grade.

- Do you want to lessen the burden of *public servants* like social workers and law enforcement officers? Teach a child to read.

- Do you want to create a better *United States of America*, no longer burdened by 20% of adults unable to read well enough to hold a living wage job? Teach the children to read.

- Do you want to lift the daily burdens of *working citizens,* make the streets safer, the prisons emptier, and the tax burden lighter? Then give children the tools to contribute.
- Do you want to help *future generations* make sure their citizenry is full of reading parents who can pass along the gift of literacy you helped provide? Help a child learn to read.

O God, restore us
And cause Your face to shine upon us,
and we will be saved.
—Psalm 80:3 (NASB)

Learn more about the need in schools:

27
THE FINANCIAL IMPACT

**As each has received a gift, use it to serve
one another, as good stewards of
God's varied grace.
—1 Peter 4:10 (ESV)**

Let's take a minute to consider the financial impact of illiteracy. This is not an easy topic. People are not dollars. However, dollars are one of the ways we communicate what we care about and it is part of our stewardship as the people of God.

Everyone has opinions about taxes, but we can all be proud when our tax dollars are used, as the apostle Paul taught, to fight evil and to defend what is good (Romans 13). And on this theme, we hope that those who are in dire circumstances are defended and supported in a just and compassionate way. This includes the illiterate and those who drop out of school and society.

In the spirit of stewardship, it is worth a brief examination of the financial impact that illiteracy, and specifically a dropout, has on all of us who are faithful taxpayers.

Again, we are talking about real people and I hope we handle this conversation with sobriety and empathy.

When considering the cost of a human being who leaves the education system unable to participate in society in a full and constructive way, it is impossible to know the total cost. There are many aspects that could be factored in.

There are *sunk costs* . . . like the estimated $15,000 per year per student we collectively spent for each year of an eventual dropout's education, unfulfilled though it may have been.

There are *lost benefits*, for instance, from that dropout's unrealized income. An adult who reads at a low level is unable to get a living wage job, which means they will possibly never contribute their part to our collective tax burden. I read that the U.S. Census Bureau estimates that dropouts earn $10,000 less yearly than high school graduates and over $36,000 less than a person holding a bachelor's degree.[39] They estimated that if all the dropouts from just the class of 2011 had earned diplomas, the nation would have benefited from an estimated

$154 billion in income (and resulting taxation) over their working lifetimes.

For the remaining space, let's set aside the sunk costs and unrealized benefits and focus on the actual cost to taxpayers over the life of a dropout.

Again, there are so many factors and so many paths that a life can take that it is functionally impossible to arrive at an exact number, but let's see what we can discern.

A study done by Northeastern University in 2009 found that a high school dropout costs taxpayers $292,000 over their lifetime.[40] This number comes from economists factoring the average total funding afforded the dropout through public services, which are funded by taxpayers.

In 2021, there were two million dropouts.[41] When you multiply two million times the $292,000 number above, these dropouts cost us over $584 billion each year (those are your tax dollars). That estimate is not adjusted for inflation, so that loss was according to 2009 dollars.

Keep in mind that these numbers are averages and for the most part they are conservative.

We befriended economist Ben Scafidi, and when he crunched the numbers and included factors such as medical care and funding the criminal justice system, it didn't take long for the numbers to climb to $1 million in public dollars spent for one hypothetical high school dropout.

All of these numbers represent people. They represent futures. They represent hopelessness for so many.

Consider this . . .

- More than 30% of 4th-graders each year read below basic levels (National Center for Education Statistics)[42]
- Two million students drop out of school each year (National Center for Education Statistics)
- High school graduation rates can be reasonably predicted by knowing someone's reading skill at the end of 3rd grade (National Research Council)[43]

Ease their pain. Ease the burden on our national budget. When we provide a future and opportunities for others, all of us benefit in so many ways.

**Honor the Lord with your wealth,
with the firstfruits of all your crops;
then your barns will be filled to overflowing,
and your vats will brim over with new wine.
—Proverbs 3:9-10**

POVERTY-INFORMED MENTORING

Blessed are those who are poor.
—Jesus

We have been students of Dr. Donna M. Beegle for years. She is one of the world's foremost experts on poverty. You can learn more from her at her organization, Communications Across Barriers (ComBarriers.com).

She reminds me that there are real causes for poverty and it's not people's personalities and choices. Real causes include housing affordability, childcare and transportation crises along with hunger, lack of access to preventative care, and lack of access to good schools and living wage jobs.

What follows are five principles we have learned that were inspired by Dr. Beegle and her teachings on poverty-informed mentoring.

Children are not stupid. Children from below the poverty line may have never been exposed to middle-class vocabulary, middle-class ideas, or middle-class ways of responding because those things have never been demonstrated. People don't learn vocabulary from going to a dictionary, they learn it by experiencing words and ideas in context, rightly used by people they trust, and who they believe care about them. Additionally, there are many types of intelligences, so it's important to find out where your reading buddy excels.

Children are different, not bad . . . and many children have different (limited) access to resources, opportunities, and the luxury to learn. If you have never lived your entire life under generational poverty, remember that their background is as different from yours as if you were befriending someone from another country. Get to know them with curiosity and wonder about how they see the world *and* what they could teach you about the world from their very different perspective. This reality has multipliers when a child is also from a different culture or race than your own.

Children are overcomers. One school district was ready to give up because of chronic tardiness. They found that no amount of "tardy slips" could improve the situation. After learning the situations their kids were coming from (like living in cars), and after growing in their poverty competency, this same district changed their policy from "tardy shaming" to "we are so glad you made it today" cards. Because of their new understanding, kids were rewarded for the feat of making it to class.

Poverty is not monolithic. The experience of living below the poverty line is as diverse as the experience of being middle class. Try to check your assumptions at the door. Bring curiosity and openness to your relationship with your reading buddy. Every person is an art museum unlike any other. What a gift it is to get to visit with your child each week.

Trauma is toxic to learning. Every child below the poverty line is not necessarily living with chronic trauma. Not at all. However, studies show that there are layers and categories of trauma that children from poverty are more apt to encounter. Harvard studies show that trauma increases developmental delays. They are toxic to the otherwise quickly growing brain, diminishing brain architecture in the areas of learning and reason. The good news is that positive interaction with a caring adult helps to rebuild brain architecture, so be patient.

Dr. Beegle says all children are children, but they live in different contexts which will shape their access to resources and the luxury to learn. This will affect their emotions, behavior, and opportunities to develop to their fullest potential.

> **Speak up for those who cannot speak
> for themselves,
> for the rights of all who are destitute.
> Speak up and judge fairly;
> defend the rights of the poor and needy.
> —Proverbs 31:8-9**

Learn more about poverty and mentoring from Dr. Donna Beegle here:

29
A KEY TO EVANGELISM

You can't God-talk inside the schools, that's part of the deal . . . however, if you volunteer, you will be able to share your faith more and more everywhere else.
—A literacy leader

Across Christianity, in every denomination, I have found that devout people of God deeply desire to tell others about their faith. Some call it evangelism. Some just love to talk about what (and Whom) they love.

Now, is volunteering in a local public school the work of the Gospel of the Kingdom of God? *Yes!*

We have already discussed how Jesus desired to see the hungry fed, the prisoner freed, and the sick healed. Literacy is one of the factors shown to keep future adults off welfare, out of prison, and away from addiction (Preventative Justice). This is all a matter of fact.

We have already discussed how Jesus calls us to love our neighbor, who is in fact a stranger and a person in need. Jesus modeled this in his interactions with the leper, the hungry on the hillside, and the woman at the well. He taught about it in his sermon in Luke 4 and in the story of the Good Samaritan.

Yet, many people appropriately ask, "What about evangelism? Can being a reading mentor be considered evangelism?"

Well, the cleanest answer is probably "No." The laws on the division of church and state are clear. The requirement of every public school volunteer program is that all volunteers leave their ideologies and personal agendas (whatever they may be) at the schoolhouse door. We serve the school in whatever way they ask and no more. ***Love without agenda.***

However, in an unexpected way, being a reading mentor can be a *key* to more evangelism.

I was recently talking to my friend Dale. Dale worked for years as a missionary. He has worked in various capacities in ministries over the decades since he returned from the mission field. Dale was telling me about how he gets into gospel conversations every day.

A KEY TO EVANGELISM

You see, Dale lives the sort of life where it seems like any conversation leads to a discussion about Jesus and God's plan for humanity and the universe.

When Dale's neighbors ask him: "What's new?" "What are you up to these days?" "What's going well with you?" or "What are you passionate about these days?" Dale's answer seems to always point the conversation toward faith.

Every question inevitably leads to a Jesus-conversation, whether it is with old friends, neighbors, or a curious store clerk.

Most Christians I meet are not like Dale. They confess to me that they rarely talk about their faith.

But what if those people were doing something like being a reading mentor? Suddenly questions like—"What are you doing these days?" "What's new?" and "What do you care about?"—all can be answered with, "Let me tell you about my reading buddy at the local school."

Your neighbor follows up, "How did you become a reading buddy?"

Your answer, "My church is volunteering with children in need, because we think this is something that Jesus cares about."

And suddenly you are off on the adventure of sharing your faith. With just a little practice, you will find that the deeply personal experience of being a reading mentor *will lead to daily opportunities to share your faith.*

> **But in your hearts revere Christ as Lord. Always be prepared to give an answer to everyone who asks you to give the reason for the hope that you have. But do this with gentleness and respect, keeping a clear conscience, so that those who speak maliciously against your good behavior in Christ may be ashamed of their slander.**
> **—1 Peter 3:15-16**

30
FORMULAS

**Blessed are those who act justly,
who always do what is right.
—Psalm 106:3**

People believe in formulas all the time. For instance, anytime we think something like, "If only X and Y could happen, then Z would result," we are thinking in formulas. Some of those formulas are true . . . but unfortunately many of them are in fact false.

Here is a formula many people believe:

Child + Classroom + Time = Educated (or Literate)

What do you think of this formula? Maybe you would like to add a few exceptions, but for the majority of children, this formula seems true. Right?

Well, for any philosophical formula to be true, one must first define the terms. So let's try to do that . . .

What do we mean by "child"?

By now you know that the word "child" is surprisingly complex. Each child comes to school with their own advantages and disadvantages. In the formula above, which child are we talking about? Does this child have a full stomach? Are they carrying trauma? Do they have a stable home?

The word "child" is complicated.

What do we mean by "time"?

When it comes to school, time involves not just the eight hours a day the school doors are open. It includes a lot more. "Time" must take into account the "pre-time" before this child ever walks through those open school doors. Was someone there to make sure they got a full night's sleep? Were they awakened in time, fed a good breakfast, and emotionally prepared for the day? "Time" must ask, did that child make it to the bus stop?

Then, once in school, "time" must take into account how many distractions happened along the way. Were there disruptions by hungry or discouraged classmates? Was that day's learning hijacked by a "live shooter drill"?

What do we mean by "classroom"?

When we think "classroom," I imagine the picture in all of our minds is pretty consistent. Can you see it? Mine looks like: little desks in neat rows, a chalkboard at the front with an alphabet banner with both uppercase and lowercase letters above, books along the windowsill, posters with inspirational words along the walls. Does your imagination look similar?

But a classroom is about more than the stage and its props; it is about the play that happens every day upon that stage.

When we sit and listen to teachers talk about the drama of the classroom, here are some direct quotes:

> "It is really difficult as a teacher to meet with students one-on-one . . . because of the distractions . . . stopping and starting all day long."

> "The responsibility of the teacher has changed . . . we are not just teachers, we are mother, counselor . . . waitress, nurse, social worker, mediator . . . psychologist . . . It is physically a challenge. It is emotionally draining."

> "For some of these kids, I am like that dad-figure in their lives, I am raising these kids . . . they are with me seven or eight hours a day."

What do you think? Does *Child + Classroom + Time = Educated?* At the very least it is not as simple as many portray it to be.

So, let's change the formulas, shall we?

Here are some new formulas to consider:

Able to Read + A Desire to Care + One Hour a Week = A Reading Mentor

Literacy + Self-Esteem + Social Support = Opportunity/Hope

Teach a child to read = Give a child a chance

31
WHY WOULDN'T I?

I was teaching a preaching class to a bunch of undergrads at a small Christian liberal arts college in my hometown. It was quite an adventure, like watching a classroom of squirrels try to learn Broadway choreography.

One of my squirreliest squirrels named Joshua got up for his mid-semester sermon and taught on "Jesus and the Other" (the random people Jesus encountered throughout the Gospels).

As an illustration, Joshua told the story of himself moving around the city of Portland, Oregon, and encountering beggars . . . beggars on the street corners, beggars at the bottom of a highway offramps, etc. They were asking for food or money . . . Joshua reflected aloud, almost like he was having the memory in real time, about how he felt in those moments. His eyes were raised up to the paneled ceiling and florescent lighting, and you could see the regret all over his face.

"I was taught . . ." Joshua shared, having forgotten about his sermon notes on the podium, "I was taught in these circumstances to pray . . . to ask God if He wanted me to give this person something and I must admit, I have rarely *heard* God say, 'Do it,' so I almost never do."

Joshua nodded and his eyes returned to his classmates and his thoughts to his notes, "Now, having soaked in the stories of Jesus . . . the way that Jesus responded to the blind man, the Samaritan woman, or the little man in the tree, I am trying to ask something different and that difference has changed everything. Instead of asking God, 'Why would I . . .' I am asking, 'Why wouldn't I?'"

As an instructor, I must admit, it was a beautiful moment. He was an awkward 20-year-old, doing his best . . . but *wow*, did he speak to my heart.

I share this with you because I treasure the memory (and the lesson), but also to point out something perhaps unexpected: a teaching like Joshua's can be easily abused.

In many ways, it is difficult to put the teachings of Jesus into practice . . . in our faith it is a very reasonable application to tell you: sell all you have and move to the other side of the world and work in a leper colony for the rest of your days. That is a reasonable application.

It is a reasonable application to say, quit your job and go to seminary, or fill up your house with orphans, or give away 90% of your wealth instead of just 10%. These are all reasonable applications and someone could come along and tell the Joshua story above and say, "Why wouldn't you?"

WHY WOULDN'T I?

That would be asking a lot, maybe more than you are able to imagine for yourself, let alone act on.

I don't know what your future holds (heck, I don't know what *my* future holds). Someday you may fall in love with a country on the other side of the world, or you may fill your home with orphans, or you may quit your job to run a nonprofit, but for most of us, those are *huge* leaps.

I find that Jesus is often not as interested in the *theoretical* huge leap as he is in the *practical* next small step.

One of the things I love about inviting people to become the new best friend to a child who is struggling to read is this:

It is a practical small next step that almost anyone can do.

And if you are 15 to 95 and if you can read, "One fish, two fish . . ." and if you can offer one hour a week, it is a simple step you could take.

The steps of a good man are ordered by the Lord: and he delighteth in his way.
—Psalm 37:23 (KJV)

You may relate to this desire to help:

PART THREE

IT'S FOR YOUR CHURCH

HE HAS SHOWN YOU, O MORTAL,
WHAT IS GOOD.
AND WHAT DOES THE LORD
REQUIRE OF YOU?
TO ACT JUSTLY AND TO LOVE MERCY
AND TO WALK HUMBLY
WITH YOUR GOD.

—MICAH 6:8

32

A TRANSFORMATIONAL CHANGE

> **Love is patient, love is kind.**
> **It does not envy . . .**
> **It does not dishonor others,**
> **it is not self-seeking . . . It always protects,**
> **always trusts,**
> **always hopes, always perseveres.**
> **—1 Corinthians 13**

At the beginning of this century a movement quietly took root and spread across the U.S.

For us it began when Jeff's church decided to become the new best friend to a struggling high school in a tough Portland neighborhood.

It started as a one-off. A single day of service. It was little more than a church field trip of kindness. Suffice it to say, everyone was surprised when 1,200 church people showed up.

What did those thousand-plus people do? Well, everything, I guess. They took on all the deferred maintenance this one Oregon underfunded school wouldn't otherwise find the time or budget to attend to. They raked leaves and planted flower beds. They fixed windows and scrubbed walls. They cleaned, painted, and restored every surface to make that space worthy again of its hundreds of inner-city students.

It was lovely. Like a swarm of benevolent locusts . . . and the church people were so inspired and transformed by the whole experience that the church took on a long-term commitment to the school. They started a dozen on-going programs and staffed the school with coaches, service providers, and mentors. This school, in one of the U.S.'s most secular cities, even provided on-site office space for church-funded staff.

In 2010, we completed a film about it called *Undivided* (link below). The film spread across the country. It was viewed at the White House by the Office of Faith-Based Initiatives and by the U.S. Department of Education.

Thousands of church leaders watched.

As a result of this and other powerful and mostly anonymous initiatives, tens of thousands of church-school partnerships sprang up across the country. In Portland, every public school found themselves with a new church

A TRANSFORMATIONAL CHANGE

best friend and cities like Detroit and Phoenix were transformed.

What did these churches do? Simply put, they did whatever was asked of them. Usually it was the stuff nobody else wanted to do: from scraping gum off benches to enormous remodeling projects. This was a movement of love . . . love without agenda.

This successful movement allowed multitudes of youth to go to school in more beautified spaces.

And while the impact was undeniable, for some churches the sustainability was flawed. In those cases, it was flawed in the following ways:

- First, over time, churches struggled *to reconcile* behaviors like "scraping gum" (a wonderful selfless act) with their desire to have the life-on-life impact that they read about in the New Testament.

- Second, churches went back year after year and do you know what they found? The gum was back, the windows were broken again, the weeds had flourished, and the dirt had returned to the walls. Many were plagued by the question, *"Are we making any real difference?"* And so churches felt like they were failing.

- Third, churches wanted to make *systemic impact*. They wanted to believe that they were transforming their neighborhoods long term. They wanted to heal the systems that perpetuate poverty and separate communities.
- Fourth, they longed to *tackle a societal issue* for which the church alone could provide the answer.

That was when we went to work, did the research, collected the wisdom of church leaders, and talked to national experts in education and justice.

What did we discover? A cause that had all the benefits of these church-school partnerships *and* accomplished all four of the desires of church leaders listed above.

We needed to make a transformational change.

Hear the whole story from Jeff Martin:

WE ARE BOOK PEOPLE

The term in Hebrew is *Am HaSefer* which simply means "people of the book."

For an unknown reason, a reason that exists in the mind and mission of God, the people of God have always had an intimate relationship with the written word.

> When the Lord finished speaking to Moses on Mount Sinai, he gave him the two tablets of the Testimony, the tablets of stone inscribed by the finger of God . . . The tablets were the work of God; the writing was the writing of God, engraved on the tablets.
> —Exodus 31:18, 32:16

The leaders and writers of the Bible refer often to the written word. They don't just refer to it, but they seem to insist those around them have the ability to read those words for themselves.

Enjoy this meditation on God's people and their love of the written word . . .

> This book of the law shall not depart out of thy mouth;
> but thou shalt meditate therein day and night,
> that thou mayest observe to do according to all that is written therein:
> for then thou shalt make thy way prosperous,
> and then thou shalt have good success.
> —Joshua 1:8 (KJV)

> And keep the charge of the Lord thy God,
> to walk in his ways,
> to keep his statutes, and his commandments,
> and his judgments, and his testimonies,
> as it is written within the law of Moses.
> —1 Kings 2:3 (KJV)

> His delight is in the law of the Lord,
> and on his law he meditates day and night.
> —Psalm 1:2 (KJV)

> Go now, write it on a tablet for them,
> inscribe it on a scroll, that for the days to come
> it may be an everlasting witness.
> —Isaiah 30:8

Suddenly the fingers of a human hand appeared
and wrote on the plaster of the wall . . .
—Daniel 5:5

Now the Berean Jews were of more noble character . . .
for they received the message with great eagerness
and examined the Scriptures every day.
—Acts 17:11

. . . the righteousness of God is revealed from faith
to faith: as it is written, The just shall live by faith.
—Romans 1:17

Because it is written, Be ye holy; for I am holy.
—1 Peter 1:15-16 (KJV)

These things I have written unto you
that believe on the name of the Son of God;
that ye may know that ye have eternal life . . .
—1 John 5:13 (KJV)

Blessed is the one who reads aloud the words of this
prophecy . . .
—Revelation 1:3

And of course . . .

We have a Savior who is called the "Word" (John 1:1). We are told that this "Word became flesh and blood and moved into the neighborhood" (John 1:14, The Message).

In the first public act of ministry, here is what the Word did:

> [Jesus] went to Nazareth,
> where he had been brought up,
> and on the Sabbath day he went into the synagogue,
> as was his custom.
> And he stood up to read.
> —Luke 4:16

The work of the people of God was birthed in schools called "synagogues." The ministry was spread through written testimony (the epistles and Gospels) and even in the New Heavens and the New Earth we will be opening books (Revelation 20).

The people of God have always been and will always be book people.

34
THE CHURCH'S LITERACY HISTORY

Go into all the world ...
—Mark 16:15

In the ninth century there lived two brothers named Cyril and Methodius. These were devout Christian men, full of faith and given the gift of education.

They were born in Thessalonica, which today is in Northern Greece. They became monks and scholars, dedicating themselves to the work of the church. In time, they were revered for their minds and were appointed as educators in many disciplines including theology and philosophy.

In those days, to the north of Greece, the lands were populated with illiterate tribes in the areas we know today as the Balkans and Eastern Europe.

These brothers in many ways were the best the early church had to offer. Already accomplished and well regarded, they took their passion, their innovation, and their intellects and became missionaries to these "uneducated" lands to the north.

And what did they do? They did what the people of God always seem to do. They listened to these foreign people.

They learned their languages.

They did the long, difficult work of creating an alphabet to capture the unique sounds and syntax of their new home. Responding to all they heard and learned, they wrote the Glagolitic alphabet, which became the written form of the Old Slavonic language, which was first used to translate the Bible into that local tongue, so all could read it.

Today, that alphabet is called Cyrillic and it is used in 50 languages, the bond of cultures and the script of schools.

They made it possible for nations and generations to read.

These missionaries, Cyril and Methodius, were the literacy fathers of nations and thus today are patron saints of Europe.

This short story is but one of thousands from the history of the Christian church.

One would be hard-pressed to find a force more passionate and impactful upon the creation, promotion, and proliferation of *reading* than the Christian church.

Just think about it.

This movement, called the Church, began in schools called synagogues, arranged around the reading from the scrolls and later, the letters of the apostles.

Fueled by the incarnational example of the Word, the Church immediately transitioned their ministry from Aramaic to the common-tongue Greek, then it was taken to all the known world and contextualized into each language.

The Church became the keeper of libraries. The desert mothers and fathers were the teachers of the first centuries. Through the Middle Ages, monasteries housed the schools and the scholars.

In the fifteenth century, Guttenberg invented the printing press, partially in response to the need for Bibles and religious materials. The proliferation of the printed word accelerated the Reformation and led to a revival of literacy.

Missionaries, like Cyril and Methodius, continued this sacred work time and again into forgotten lands. In more recent times, one Christian organization, called Wycliffe Bible Translators, exists to "develop alphabets, help preliterate people learn to read and write . . . by developing written languages, the organization is helping to save lost and dying languages." They have been involved in language creation and translation in 2,500 languages where they have then provided the Bible and ongoing literacy programs.

In U.S. history, almost every small town began with a church that also served as a school at its center. Within the "parish model" of churches, even in big cities, every neighborhood had a parish church which was responsible for a parish school, schools that existed to serve *every* child within the parish. Many of these schools are still in service today.

Most of the great American universities began as Christian missions and many still have a chapel at the center of their campuses.

Sunday school was originally created as the only place for impoverished peoples to learn to read.

I have been asked time and again, "Why should the church get involved in the literacy business?"

I ask you, "When did the church *stop* being the leader of the literacy business?"

Let's lead again.

Watch how one church in Detroit joined this 2000 year old story:

35
CONFESSION

Forgive us for what we have done and for what we have left undone.
—The Book of Common Prayer

Back in 2002, I was working at an infamously reclusive and academic college, whose unofficial motto was, "Atheism, Communism, Free Love." I was not there in an official capacity. There were a handful of Christian students on campus who were kind enough to let me hang out with them and support them. The entire campus was populated by radical activists and this small group of Christian students were just as radical.

To celebrate the end of every school year there is a spirited and overly expressive festival. These Christian students wanted to participate and they wanted, like all the other students, to bring their ideology (faith) to bear.

I won't bore you with the long creative process we went through, but finally, as a close-knit group of believers, we decided we would build a free-standing confession booth, right in the middle of the festivities, somewhere between the detox tent, the hallucination room, and the pirate ship they built for the fire/water battle . . . (on reflection, a free-standing plywood box next to a fire battle was probably not the wisest move).

The idea for the confession booth was simple. The students asked me to dress as a monk, to sit on one side of the booth and they would invite students to enter by cheering, "Confessions being heard! Come, enter!"

Once a student entered, I, dressed in my clerical garb, would say something like this, "Welcome. In this space confessions are heard and if it is all right with you, I would like to begin. I am a Christian and Christianity has been responsible for many things that need forgiveness. My religious family perpetrated the Crusades and the Inquisition. We have contributed time and again to slavery, racism, and war . . ." This confession would go on for some time and would end with, "and I personally don't live up to the example my master Jesus modeled. I don't love you students unconditionally and sacrificially. I am judgmental . . . would you please forgive *me* for my sins and for the sins of my religious family?"

It was one of the scariest things I have ever done.

And you know what happened next? Every time, the student (or students) who had piled into that little plywood space, would say, "I forgive you. I forgive you for all of it."

And then they would confess their pain . . . abuse, loneliness, addiction. We would sit together in the sacred candlelight and care for each other's souls.

Why do I tell you this story?

I tell you because that weekend festival, and those dozens of students who forgave me, was one of the most transformational experiences of my life. There is a release of invisible shackles when one confesses aloud and admits that, on some level, we share responsibility for the mistakes of our family, even our historical spiritual family.

I believe that the Christian church has been the most impactful force for good for bringing reading to the nations over the last 2,000+ years . . . but, at the same time, our education record is not without dark and shameful chapters.

It does not take long for any of us to think of stories or news articles where church people have harmed children in their tender school years . . . stories of innocence betrayed and destroyed. Which stories come to your mind?

The story that jumps immediately to my mind is this: God gave me a Native American mentor. I called him Uncle Richard (he passed in 2013). Uncle Richard loved Jesus and yet he would tearfully lament to me the challenges he had in forgiving the Christian church . . . for the cultural, physical, and emotional abuse so many Indigenous children endured in reservation religious schools. Countless children ripped from their families, amputated from their culture, emotionally shredded by the worst kinds of abuses, and many assaulted even to the point of death.

This story is a part of my religious family's history. *I confess the evil done by my spiritual family. Forgive us for our sins.*

> **Confess your faults one to another . . .**
> **—James 5:16 (KJV)**

There is nothing we can do to right these wrongs or to even adequately apologize for them . . .

But we can confess the sins of our spiritual family and the countless children who our people have harmed.

And we can choose to do better.

> **We can care for children in the right way**
> **moving forward . . . forgotten children,**
> **marginalized children, the children**
> **who Jesus loves.**

Watch Tony tell the Confession Booth story:

GOD LOVES JUSTICE

**Evildoers do not understand what is right,
but those who seek the Lord
understand it fully.
—Proverbs 28:5**

In the city of Detroit, we have a friend named Doug Kempton. You would love Doug. He is the real thing.

Doug has spent much of his adult life caring for under-resourced kids. He has started sports programs in forgotten neighborhoods. He has sponsored mentoring. And he started a literacy nonprofit called "SOAR Detroit."

Doug is a hero. He cares for kids in a way that I don't believe I could ever emulate.

When talking to Doug about his work, he made this surprising confession to me . . .

We were three years into the program and I was tutoring a young boy—and I'd been serving kids in the city for 12 years by then. I just had this realization sitting across from this young man that he was smart. I actually thought to myself, this kid's as smart as my kid. The problem with that is I believed something, right? *There was a prejudice in me that I didn't even know existed.* And there I sat with this little boy and realized that there's something dark about what I believe; that because he was black, he wasn't as smart as my kid. How sick is that?

If a hero like Doug can be that self-aware and confess that he still has so far to go to activate the unprejudiced heart that God wants him to have . . . how far must my heart need to go?

The prophet Ezekiel lamented:

I looked for someone among them who would build up the wall and stand in the gap on behalf of the land . . . but I found no one.

—Ezekiel 22:30

The prophet is lamenting two things at once. He is lamenting a literal gap that someone needs to volunteer and fill in order to keep the people from grave peril. He is also talking about a gap in the people's hearts. He cries out for someone to fulfill the desires of the Father's heart and no one would answer the call.

Another friend we met in Detroit is named Marquise. Marquise grew up unable to read, but later in life got some help, and that help, coupled with his love for God, has him volunteering as a reading mentor in his local school. He is trying to stand in the gap.

Marquise said to me:

> I know there are a lot of churches that will want to come back and help and give. That is definitely a good thing. But I think the church people will really be surprised when they get out here in what I call the trenches. Not only are they going to be helping to fix the problem, *but they're going to get fixed.* They're going to get helped. Because sometimes in a church there's a sense of, oh, we got it right and they don't, which Jesus is not happy with that. You know what I'm saying?

That is a lot to take in. While we process that, also consider a few more words from our friend, Doug Kempton:

> If I had a message, it's that we have a chance to actually change a broken system. And the broken education system is the quintessential definition of injustice. And

if God says, "I love justice," then the church is going to have to step into the injustice and make a difference in this broken education system.

Like Ezekiel, Doug is pointing to an unjust societal gap that someone is going to need to fill. And maybe by filling it, the gap in our hearts will be healed as well.

> **To do righteousness and justice is more acceptable to the Lord than sacrifice . . .**
> **It is a joy for the just to do justice.**
> **—Proverbs 21:3,15 (NKJV)**

Watch more from Doug Kempton here:

CHANGE THE WORLD

> **Live an exemplary life in your neighborhood so that your actions will refute their prejudices. Then they'll be won over to God's side and be there to join in the celebration when he arrives.**
> **—1 Peter 2:12 (The Message)**

I was raised to believe that I could change the world. I thought that was what being a Christian was all about. Maybe that is just a young person's way of thinking . . . maybe it is naive to think one can change the world.

Something happened along the way. I am not sure what it was. It was probably a whole series of changes. I learned that I am not invincible. I started to have bills to pay and responsibilities to keep. I became more worried about my family, my mortgage, and my retirement. Maybe this happens to everyone, but my faith slowly became more and more theoretical. It became more about thinking about *what* I believe and less about *acting on* what God cares about.

One of the reasons that this literacy work has been so fulfilling for us is because churches get to enact real change. They get to witness changed lives and activated futures.

We tell pastors that it is a perfect beginning level of commitment to invite your people into. You don't have to ask your people for more money. You don't have to ask them to open their home to people they don't know. They don't need to acquire a radical new skill set. You don't have to ask them to rearrange their schedules beyond finding one lunch hour a week.

You might say, it is a gateway-activity into a lifestyle of justice and compassion.

The other thing about it is this: we, the U.S. church, *could actually change the country.*

Try and think of another tragic issue that the U.S. church could actually, practically, and measurably change. Any ideas?

Well, we could sell all of our church properties and pay off the nation's school or medical debt. We could open all our homes and end the immigration crisis. We could all quit our jobs and join Habitat for Humanity. Those are all good ideas, but I am not sure most of us are prepared for that level of sacrifice. Is that too blunt?

However, if every school had a church partner, and a portion of that church's people gave up one hour a week to be reading mentors, illiteracy in the country could be functionally cured. Cured!

According to WorldAtlas.com, the U.S. ranks 125th in literacy (Finland is first). There are many ways to gauge something like literacy, but 125th! One hundred and twenty-four countries are more literate than we are?!

Now imagine this. We could all wake up in a few years and the illiteracy crisis could be over. No longer would one in three children in 4th grade read below basic levels. No longer would one in five adults be powerless to acquire a living wage job because they can't read. And *we* could do it. We could erase this *one issue*. And that would change the country.

There are 65,000 elementary schools in the U.S. and there are almost 400,000 churches. Do you know what every neighborhood, every village, and every frontier outpost has? A school and a few churches.

We could do this.

We wouldn't have to sell our churches, sublet our homes, or quit our jobs to do it either.

We just need to have compassion on the "least of these" for one hour a week.

Learn more about US literacy history here:

38
CHURCHES ARE THE BEST

It is hard to imagine a group of people who are better prepared for radical goodness.

Think about it. Every Sunday morning, parades of people migrate together into local churches to sit and prepare for radical goodness.

We sing the songs of God about heavenly goodness, truth, and beauty.

Our leaders give testimony to the wonderful works of God's people both locally and around the world.

Our pastors remind us of the Scripture's call to love God and love our neighbor.

And at the end of the service, most communities end with a dismissal blessing that literally endows all those present to catalyze radical goodness. Something like:

> Go. You are called to worship God, to show forth Christ, and, in the power of the Holy Spirit, to be a

vital presence in the lives of your neighbors, families, and the community. Amen.

Radical goodness is the indisputable intention of the people of God. Now, considering all the ways to do good, why focus that goodness on helping children read?

Well, it is not the only way . . . but it may be a cause for which the church is best equipped.

The church is . . .

The Best at Kids

I have assisted in planting dozens of churches. In so many, the first big hire is the "youth pastor." Why? Because kids are our priority. How many other organizations act like this? When you walk through your church, how much of the square footage is dedicated to caring for children—from the nursery to the Sunday school rooms to the play spaces?

It is already a huge part of church budgets, energy, and prayers. Churches are already the best at kids.

The Best at Fun

Where to start: Sunday school skits, summer camp, Vacation Bible School, silly songs, and midweek Bible clubs. When I was a kid, I went to Church Olympics and was a member of a Bible Quiz team.

Inside a church's walls are incubated more expressions of healthy and empowering fun than maybe any other place on earth. Let's share those gifts outside the church's walls.

The Best at Stories

Just walk into the nursery on any given Sunday. Stand for just a moment and watch. You will find an army of radical goodness with a book in one hand and a baby cradled in the other.

Sunday school classrooms, missionary reports, and sermon illustrations are all full of the art of storytelling.

The Best at Mentoring

I remember very early on being introduced to the idea of "multiplication." I read Robert Coleman's famous book, *The Master Plan of Evangelism*, where he reminded everyone that Jesus's plan was to pour his life into just 12 people.

2 Timothy 2:2 was the model:

And the things you have heard me say in the presence of many witnesses entrust to reliable people who will also be qualified to teach others.

Paul's plan:
Paul —> Timothy —> reliable people —> others

It is no doubt that literacy mentoring in a public school limits what a mentor can do or say, but it does allow Christians to use their mentoring skills to bless others.

It is hard to imagine a group of people who have been more divinely equipped to populate a reading movement than the Church.

Church: Great at kids, fun, stories, and mentoring.

Watch the story of how one church got involved:

39
FOR OUR PLACE AND TIME

Eugene Peterson does this interesting thing with John 1:14. He translates it as:

> **The Word became flesh and blood and moved into the neighborhood.**

I find that provocative.

Theologians spill gallons of ink talking about incarnational theology. That is a five-syllable word that could be simply defined: living in the neighborhood, living for the neighborhood, living like your neighborhood.

Hudson Taylor was a nineteenth-century missionary to China. He broke all the rules by following Jesus's neighborhood example and dressed like the people, acted like the people, and talked in the language of the people of his place and time: pre-modern China.

It is an important theological idea that Jesus did not become a "global human." Jesus became a Nazarene, a Galilean. They called him that because they could tell: he had the mannerisms of his home, he (like Peter in Mark

14:70) had a Galilean accent, he probably even smelled like the particular goat cheese they ate in Galilee.

By extension, each of us is called to be the "Galilean" of our particular place and time. I am not called to be a global Christian. I am called to be a Portlandian Christian, for the sake of the Kingdom of God in my place. And you are called to be the _____ Christian of your place and time. And the more we speak like, in, and for our place, the more our place will be able to hear us. Then they might believe that we are for them and love them.

Because of this foundational and paramount theological ideal, early churches organized themselves as parishes. This meant that each church literally took responsibility for their particular time and place. They drew lines and said, "Whatever happens here is our responsibility. We take responsibility for the spiritual, emotional, and physical needs of this population of people." It was an ecclesiastical (church organizing) principle that defined the spiritual community. And the belief was that, if every church took responsibility for their time and place, *no one* would be left uncared for. To God be the glory.

The modern church has lost this foundational ideal.

In our secularized society, churches struggle to manifest this parish passion perhaps because so much of the feeding, helping the homeless, and counseling work has been surrendered to civil systems.

Lesslie Newbigin, in his must-read book, *The Gospel in a Pluralist Society*, describes the future of the church as:

> ... a community that does not live for itself but is deeply involved in the concern of its neighborhood. It will be the church for the specific place where it lives ... it is God's embassy in a specific place.

Our impact may not be found in creating more church programs or even devising more congregational education. The opportunity to transform the hearts of both clergy and laity will only happen through life-on-life connection with the people of your parish.

The Holy Spirit, in wisdom and creativity, has created a wide-open doorway to reimagine parish life through literacy. Now, if only we have the vision to walk through.

Many churches find realizing Newbigin's vision of being "God's embassy in a specific place" confounding and discouraging. Take heart. It does not need to be discouraging.

The Word longs to be made flesh and blood again *in you and your church* **and move, once again,** *into the neighborhood.* **To God be the glory.**

40
FULL DEPLOYMENT

> **Jesus appointed seventy-two others and sent them two-by-two.**
> —Luke 10:1

One of the greatest challenges to pastors is to get everyone involved. How do you get people out of the pews? How do you inspire action? And sadly, what do you do with the too often overlooked folks in every congregation?

At the same time, one of the reasons why many congregants leave church is for reasons like:

I never really found my role.

My talents were not appreciated.

I didn't feel like I belonged.

We believe that in almost every church, there are whole networks of people who have not found their place. We are not talking about the 10% of the church who already teach Sunday school, serve on church boards, or help deliver the Sunday worship service. We are talking about all the others.

Of course, we believe that literacy is one of the most transformative, long-term impacting, and hope-infusing programs that any church could commit to.

We also believe that literacy is a mobilizing superhighway for your entire congregation, even those who might otherwise feel neglected or overlooked.

Here are a few examples:

Grandmas and Grandpas

They may be well past their camp counseling and youth group rousing days, but they know that they still have much to offer. Who better to be a reading mentor than someone who has free time in the middle of the day, knows better than anyone what is most important in life, *and* just happens to have spent a lifetime reading books to children and grandchildren?

Grandpas and Grandmas are an untapped goldmine for the next generation.

Stay-at-Home Parents

Once those toddlers grow a little and head off to preschool, that house can feel really empty and *really* quiet.

Sure, the new privacy might be a nice reprieve, but eventually, everyone needs to know that they are making a difference.

Certainly, parents have a bunch of responsibilities, but a one-hour break, to walk down to the public school once a week and be a reading mentor, might be just what the doctor ordered. They can put their well-honed book reading skills into loving a "stranger."

Teenagers

We like to say that being a reading mentor is the perfect work for anybody 17-75 years old, but really the number expands beyond that. There are teenagers (sometimes ones who don't feel like the "cool kids") who want to serve. Be they academic, activistic, or apathetic, being the new best friend to a 9-year-old might be just the thing they need.

As we travel the country, we are thrilled to witness that teenagers are often the most effective reading mentors in a local program.

Now pastors, it is part of your calling to bring meaning to the lives of *all* of your congregants, even those who are too often overlooked.

There is one more amazing thing that happens when your church starts a literacy initiative for your congregants:

All those grandmas and parents and teenagers . . . and businesspeople and church staff and swing-shift workers . . . and, and, and . . . they will stop thinking about leaving the church and instead start to say:

I have a role.

I am appreciated.

I belong.

And your church will be stronger and more activated because of it.

GROW YOUR CHURCH

If you are a church leader, odds are you have books on your shelf, notebooks in your file cabinet, and invitations to conferences in your inbox all about "How to grow your church."

It is a big issue. In fact, some people's job security relies upon it.

We don't claim to be experts in the industry of church growth and therefore we will not bore you with heavy-handed words about the necessity or theory of expanding your numbers, your coffers, or your facilities. Instead, we want to suggest *three simple ways* that a literacy initiative will undoubtedly strengthen your flock.

1. Leadership Development

Every pastor we talk to laments some version of "10% of my church is shouldering 95% of the work." This happens for a number of reasons. Some people feel like they don't have the knowledge, like a seminary degree, to really lead in the church. Other people struggle to see themselves as important enough or valued enough to serve. And still others are scared to commit the time.

A literacy initiative provides a bevy of little leadership roles for people to grow their leadership skills. You could select volunteer coordinators, site leaders, and communications directors for your movement. Not to mention, every reading mentor is getting on-the-job training in teaching, activism, and coaching.

2. Our-Church-Reads Evangelism

Sadly, churches grow because other churches shrink or close, denominational devotees move to town, or simply because people are fickle. How much of your church growth comes because of evangelism? It is the holy grail of growth, isn't it? Or is that too much to hope for?

Church congregants complain they don't know how to talk to their neighbors about their faith nor how to invite them to church. The great thing about being a reading mentor is that it is a zero-anxiety way to bring up one's faith.

Neighbor: "What have you been up to?"

Congregant: "Fantastic stuff: I've been reading weekly with this great kid named Billy."

Neighbor: "How did you get into that?"

Congregant: "Our church is helping dozens of kids in local schools who might not learn to read otherwise. We believe it is the kind of thing Jesus would do . . ."

And off the conversation goes. From there, any one of your people could talk about their faith journey, describe how their faith affects their life, invite their neighbor to come to church, or join their church as a reading mentor.

3. Strengthen Your Reputation

Every year, the United States increasingly becomes a post-Christian country. The statistics are irrefutable: fewer and fewer people are attending church and fewer and fewer are calling themselves Christians.

This is happening for more reasons than we have room to discuss here, but one of the reasons is that the church is seen by outsiders as irrelevant. They perceive it as little more than a tradition or a social club with no real-world import or impact. This of course could not be farther from the truth, but the problem is they don't get to *see* all the good the church does.

Paul tells Timothy about a church leader:

**They must have a good reputation
with outsiders.**

One amazing aspect of a church literacy program in an under-resourced school is that it will happen on the public stage. Schools are everyone's concern and schools impact everyone's lives. That is why there are so many local news stories about schools. Put your church inside a neighborhood school and people will notice.

Teach kids to read and grow your church.

42
OTHER PEOPLE'S MONEY

At a reading-mentor gathering, a parishioner asked his pastor, "How much did this literacy program cost the church?"

To which the pastor answered, "Well, I don't know. How much did that case of bottled waters over there cost?"

Money. Sheesh! How much church energy goes into dealing with money? The collecting of money. The strategizing about money. The distribution of money. The saying "no" to important things because there is *not enough money*.

When we survey pastors, time and time again they say some version of, "If only we could remove the question of money from the equation, think of all we could do!"

Church leaders are creative, passionate, and entrepreneurial people. In every department of their community, if given just a few minutes, most leaders could conjure up a dozen great ideas or new programs to start. The problem is that each new program or idea costs money . . . and there are only so many dollars in the coffer.

But does it have to be that way?

I imagine that the disciples had to worry about money from time to time. When you think about it, they probably had a really talented board of trustees, what with a former tax collector, some small business owners, and Judas "the keeper of the money purse" (John 12:6). I'm sure the money question was well tended to.

At the same time, Jesus was surprisingly willing to simply use other people's money (or resources), instead of dipping into the disciples' money purse.

If Jesus needed a donkey, he just borrowed one.

If he needed a room for a banquet, he just used some unnamed person's upper room.

If he needed to feed 5,000 of his closest friends, he just took a kid's lunch.

His revival meetings and evangelistic events were planned in free spaces like courtyards, hillsides, and public squares.

Heck, when he needed to pay taxes, he took a coin from a fish (Matthew 17:27).

Like all of us, they could not ignore the question of money, but when available, Jesus seemed very astute at using other people's money.

So here is one crazy thing about literacy. In many cases, a church literacy initiative will add near zero dollars to the church's budget.

My city, Portland, Oregon, is one of the most unchurched cities in the U.S. with one of the least-Christian populations. It is crazy to think that when a church here decides to start a literacy program in an under-resourced school, *that program is already paid for.*

What was that? Yes, it's already paid for!

By whom? Well, just like in most every city in the U.S., there already exists a literacy organization that is *desperate for volunteers.* This organization is already fully funded . . . funded by the progressive local government and by donations from predominantly non-church people.

Incredibly, this organization is actually over-funded. They are functioning at a fraction of their capacity and meeting only a small percentage of the need.

At the same time, this literacy organization has already taken care of all of the politics. They already have all of the strategic relationships. They have already set the programs in place. They have already funded the administration staff. They have already created the training.

And they will pay for all the necessary procedures like background checks.

Normally, when starting a new program, a church would have to research, network, organize, and *pay for* all these processes.

Now, if only we could get a fish to pay our taxes.

When your church adopts a school—to make sure that every "least of the students" receives the vital gifts of literacy, hope, and self-esteem—you will get to mobilize dozens of congregants, and do so with near zero impact on your coffers.
It's crazy but it's true.

43
AND IT MIGHT CHANGE EVERYTHING

> **Now to him who is able to do immeasurably
> more than all we ask or imagine, according
> to his power that is at work within us, to
> him be glory in the church and in Christ
> Jesus throughout all generations,
> for ever and ever! Amen.**
> **—Ephesians 3:20-21**

We are constantly amazed by the power that comes from great leadership.

At a little church we had never heard of in Waco, Texas, we met a charming woman of Hispanic descent named Stephanie. This was years ago when we were just starting to learn about how deep the cracks of illiteracy run in our country *and* the potential generational impact that local churches could provide.

It is hard to remember exactly how we heard about Stephanie, but we knew we wanted to learn her story.

Her church is called Antioch. She had been asked to run a little literacy program out of the church that was serving a handful of kids at a local school. By this point in this book, you can imagine what we are talking about when we say "literacy program:" local volunteers sitting with under-privileged kids in a school setting. Stephanie's plan was "book clubs." Clubs meant a room of little circles comprised of one adult and three kids all working together on their reading comprehension.

You might say Stephanie is a dreamer. Can you relate?

Stephanie increased the program's professionalism and they quickly started to grow. And as a dreamer, Stephanie's passion inspired her to serve the three most under-resourced schools with the three lowest reading performance scores in the district.

She refined their system. She recruited the volunteers out of Antioch. She expanded their impact. And within seven years, those three schools from Waco's poorest neighborhoods became the *highest*-scoring schools in the district.

Today, her program, called STARS, is serving 21 schools with 300 volunteers from a couple dozen churches, all coordinated and paid for as a church ministry.

Stephanie is now on the Waco school board and influencing literacy programs all across the nation.

Stephanie is not alone.

AND IT MIGHT CHANGE EVERYTHING

Roy Chang is in Seattle. His Chinese Alliance Church sat across the street from an under-performing local school.

In 2004, his church began by sharing parking lots and distributing waters and cookies after school. But that wasn't enough for Pastor Roy, nor was it enough for Dearborn School . . . so a partnership was born.

Seattle Chinese Alliance (SCA) became the go-to phone call for school families in need. They hosted a monthly community meal, provided clothing and school supplies and sponsored campus clean-up days.

In time, an everyday after-school program was born for low-income, mostly BIPOC (Black, Indigenous, People of Color) students, providing literacy and homework support.

Because of the work of SCA church, today Pastor Roy oversees School Connect Washington and is bringing school support, often through church partnerships, all across the Seattle area. He was just awarded a substantive grant to support the after-school program at Dearborn Park Elementary.

Today, Pastor Herman Greene's church is in the Saint Johns neighborhood of North Portland, among low-income communities. After decades of serving in dozens of ways to try and bring equity and opportunity back to the children of his neighborhood, Pastor Herman has started an after-school reading program. He has become a member of the local school board and, because of his growing impact, he and his church have been tasked with creating a literacy model to help inspire the entire state of Oregon.

All this to say . . . you may dip your toe in a literacy mentoring program for any one of many reasons. Maybe because it started out not costing much money or because you were inspired by the work of *preventative justice*, or maybe you just wanted your people to practice loving their forgotten neighbors.

Whatever the reason, don't be surprised if your new literacy mentoring program explodes into much more than you ever asked or imagined.

Watch Stephanie tell more of her story in Waco:

44
MAKING HISTORY

> **He healed all the sick, warning them
> not to tell who He was.**
> **—Matthew 12:15**

In the chapter called "A Transformational Change," we told you the story of a lovely church that adopted a struggling inner-city high school. We shared with you about a one-off clean-up day that turned into a decade-long relationship between a school in a liberal U.S. city and a comparatively conservative church.

Confession: we didn't tell you the whole story.

Yes, the relationship continued to grow. And it was amazing . . . including clothes closets, mentoring programs, and many more clean-up days. The church, however, did not stop there.

You see, although this church was not huge, they did have some privilege, more than most. They just happened to have some powerful congregants and friends who have influence in some of the city's most powerful companies. This church worked the phones, built the partnerships, and (among other things) gave that high school's sports program a massive facelift. When I say facelift, I mean turning an all but unusable football field into a state-of-the-art sports arena (track, football field, etc.) that was so advanced, it is now the home of statewide championships.

This school, which before this church relationship began was probably on the state closure list, is now regarded as a gem in the school system's crown.

Okay, here is the tough truth: Today, when the school district or the city tells the story of the school's transformation, who do you think almost never gets mentioned? Who doesn't get the credit?

The church.

To be sure the district and the city were necessary partners in this transformation story . . . but today, this church stands in the shadows and allows others to write the history books. When that history is recounted, it no longer includes their tens of thousands of volunteer hours or their hundreds of thousands of donated dollars or the avalanche of love this church unleashed on this otherwise forgotten school.

It hurts to be forgotten.

MAKING HISTORY 211

Jesus went on healing spates that sometimes get lost in the Bible narrative. In addition to the stories of individual healings (blind man, leper, demoniac, etc.), there are many times the writers get lazy and just say: "So Jesus went through and He healed everyone, it was a miracle tsunami" (paraphrase of Matthew 4:23-24; 8:16-17; 9:35; 12:15; 14:14, 34-36; 15:29-31; 19:2 and 21:14).

That's a lot of healing.

What do you think happened after Jesus left one of these villages?

I imagine a scene where a traveler might wander through one of these tsunami-healed villages and find the local rabbi and inquire, "Holy smokes, there seems to be a lot of religious fervor in this village. The people really seem to love God." To which the rabbi might answer, "Simple traveler, what you are witnessing is the fruit of my many years of tireless teaching of the Scriptures and my humble prayers for my people."

In this fictional story, God did answer the rabbi's prayers, even if the rabbi forgot to mention Jesus.

We have heard many tales of churches doing incredible work, and in the end, when the history books were written, someone else took all the credit.

Sometimes there are hurt feelings.

We tell you this because we don't want you to be surprised. It might happen to you.

Also, we want to invite you into the elegant and often anonymous work of the Kingdom of God . . . wherein, ultimately, it doesn't matter who gets credit. It doesn't matter what the other history books say, because . . .

Your history will be written on the lives of the children to whom you offer a future and a hope. Your history book will be the empty prison cells, the shortened welfare lines, and the future parents who will be able to give the gifts of learning and hope to their children.

The pages of your history will be transformed homes, renewed neighborhoods, and healed systems of justice. To God be the glory.

Watch the whole *Undivided* story here:

45
BELONGING

> "For I know the plans I have for you,"
> declares the Lord, "plans to prosper you
> and not to harm you,
> plans to give you hope and a future."
> —Jeremiah 29:11

We are approaching this book's conclusion, and across these pages, we have hardly used the word "belonging." It is a powerful word. And it is a powerful theme of a life-on-life mission like mentoring.

In Part One, "It's for the *Children*," almost every chapter touched on belonging in one or more ways. We tried to explain scripturally, statistically, and anecdotally how succeeding in reading and school provides the hope of healthy belonging and rescues children from the destruction of false belonging.

We discussed what happens when an adult enters a hurting child's life and says, "I'm here for you, you have a future." What happens when the classroom becomes a place where a marginalized child now belongs. What happens when the feelings of rejection are removed. What happens when they feel like welcomed participants in society.

It is reasonable to look at the children and feel compassion and even responsibility for their plight . . . an empathy that compels you to get involved.

But to you church leaders, while feeling concern for the children, please don't forget to also look inside the walls of your church family.

We met Mary in a large Midwest city. She was a beautiful and open-hearted older woman who comfortably carried her wrinkles into our interview.

She told us about her loss: "I shook him and said, 'Are you okay,' and there was no response." Her tears began to flow and she quickly wiped them away. "I must admit, I almost gave up. I was very close to giving up. I don't remember the first year and a half after he died. I was to a point where I couldn't really function . . . that's why I believe in God, because something pulled me out."

Mary was so generous with her pain and loneliness. Her humility washed over the room like she knew her life was a testimony to God's grace.

"You want to find a purpose. What is my purpose now? That's where this mentorship comes in. I never want to be this stereotype of some white lady saving the world; that is not what this is about. This is for me to help myself by helping other people."

We have a crisis of loneliness in the U.S. today. It is pervasive. It affects every demographic and statistically, churchgoers struggle almost as much.

> In 2020, Harvard reported 61% of young adults and 51% of mothers with young children feel "serious loneliness."[44]
>
> In 2023, the U.S. Surgeon General reported the highest levels of loneliness and isolation among people with poor physical or mental health, disabilities, financial insecurity, those who live alone, single parents, as well as younger and older populations.[45]
>
> In 2023 published research, Johns Hopkins reported that socially isolated older adults had a higher chance of developing dementia.[46]
>
> Churches are among society's best hope to foster healing and connection. We celebrate the work that you do in providing small groups, home Bible studies, socials, eldercare, visitations, and community ministries. Thank you for all you do.

Beyond that, we will leave you with these words from our humble and honest friend Mary:

"I feel like I'm being selfish doing this (mentoring) because of how much it is helping me . . . if that's all I do for the rest of my life, then so be it . . . so be it."

For none of us lives for ourselves alone, and
none of us dies for ourselves alone. If we
live, we live for the Lord; and if we die,
we die for the Lord.
So, whether we live or die,
we belong to the Lord.
—Romans 14:7-8

Watch Mary's story here:

46
PRACTICING FOR HEAVEN

> **We get so insulated in our Christian bubble that we never really walk with anyone who is different.**
> **—Stephanie Korteweg,**
> **Waco, TX**
> **Literacy Activist**

I think God might just have a diversity agenda. It is just a thought, but how else would you explain the reason for Acts 2? It is the first day, the birthday of the Church, and what does the Spirit of God do? The Spirit immediately particularizes the Christian message in almost every known language of the ancient world:

> God-fearing Jews from every nation under heaven . . . each one heard their own language being spoken . . . Parthians, Medes and Elamites; residents of Mesopotamia, Judea and Cappadocia, Pontus and

Asia, Phrygia and Pamphylia, Egypt and the parts of Libya near Cyrene; visitors from Rome; Cretans and Arabs. "We hear them declaring the wonders of God in our own tongues!"

—Acts 2:5-11

It is like the Holy Spirit knew the end of the story and decided we might as well jumpstart the plan from day one. How do we know that this was the plan? Perhaps because we get a glimpse of the story's end in Heaven:

> After this I looked, and there before me was a great multitude that no one could count, from every nation, tribe, people, and language, standing before the throne and before the Lamb.
>
> —Revelation 7:9

If we know how the story began and we know how the story climaxes, why wouldn't we want to practice God's plan in our churches today?

And yet so many of us don't.

Dr. Martin Luther King Jr. famously said in 1960:

Eleven o'clock on Sunday morning is one of the most segregated hours, if not the most segregated hour, in Christian America.

I am sad to bear witness that MLK's sentiment is still true. I have traveled the country and spoken to hundreds of pastors, and over and over again, they confess their discouragement about failing to diversify their congregations. Even more so, they have no idea about how to inspire their congregations to bring Heaven's diversity into their daily lives.

The reality is that most of us surround ourselves with people who come from similar backgrounds to ours . . . they look like us, live like us, think like us, read like us, vote like us, spend like us, and worship like us. Many confess a total inability to make a friend from a distinctly different background.

Even those who can cite some diverse friendships admit that those relationships are the exception, not the rule. They would love to know more.

Well, if you are a pastor or a caring parishioner, and if you would like to create a potential superhighway to diverse friendships for your people, there is a solution that will not surprise you if you have read this far into this book.

Odds are, many of your reading mentor volunteers will be placed with a child from a radically divergent background. Their reading buddy will likely come from a different racial, cultural, or economic community. I can guarantee that they will be from a different stage of life.

Building diverse community as God models in Acts 2 and Revelation 7 can feel like an impossible challenge, but remember . . .

There is nothing intimidating about a 9-year-old.

47
FOLLOW ME

Come, follow Me.
—Jesus

There is a simple way to describe the way that Jesus lived. I would hate to call it a ritual and I certainly don't want to franchise it, but it seems to me that there are four simple steps.

Step One: KNOW the Pain

From his youngest of years, we have evidence that Jesus was a student of what his heavenly father cares about. By the age of 12, the Scriptures say that his understanding was such that everyone who heard him was amazed (Luke 2:47).

Just to drive the point home, before Jesus ever performed a miracle or gave a sermon, in Luke, we find him reading from the Scriptures about his father's heart:

> The Spirit of the Lord is on me,
> because he has anointed me
> to proclaim good news to the poor.
> He has sent me to proclaim freedom for the prisoners
> and recovery of sight for the blind,
> to set the oppressed free,
> to proclaim the year of the Lord's favor.
> —Luke 4:17-19

Step Two: SEE the Person

With his heart and mind full of the knowledge of what God cares about, Jesus set out into the world and there was able to *see* people all around him, people that others seemed blind to. He lived his life along the highways and byways, wherever the forgotten collected . . . and be they sitting in a tree, lowered through a roof, alone at a well, or wailing at the side of the road, Jesus saw them.

There is a special sort of magic that comes with starting to actually see. Seeing leads to caring in a way that knowing can't do on its own. How many people do you know who never really cared about an issue until it affected someone they truly saw . . . like a friend or a family member? It is like when someone goes on an international mission trip. They see the people, and from that day forward, that people group remains their forever favorite.

Step Three: PARTICIPATE in God's Work

I am sure the leper would have had the best day of his life if all he experienced was a famous rabbi who took a break from his day, came over, acknowledged him, touched his shoulder, and said a blessing. I am sure, for the leper, that would have been a banner day. But Jesus didn't stop there.

Jesus *participated* in the healing work of God . . . and a life was changed forever.

Step Four: Do It TOGETHER

We would hardly be the first people to point out that Jesus rarely did any acts of compassion alone. He always had someone with him. And when he didn't, like the Samaritan woman at the well in John 4, it didn't take long for his team to show up.

Jesus also seemed to never send people out alone and the apostles followed Jesus's example:

> In Acts 3:1-10, armed with all Jesus had taught them over the last three years (*know*), Peter and John (*together*) went into the temple courts and what did they *see*? "A man lame from birth" (verse 2). It says, "Peter looked straight at him, as did John" (verse 4). It says that the man wanted money, but Peter and John instead *participated* in the healing work of the Father.

The result: "He jumped to his feet and began to walk. Then he went with them into the temple courts, walking and jumping, and praising God" (verse 8).

Know – See – Participate – Together

I have some great news—when it comes to the issue of illiteracy, you have already completed the first step. After reading this book (isn't literacy a gift?), you now *know* quite a bit about illiteracy and its devastating impact on children (and also the hope and healing that the gift of reading can bring).

Only three more steps to go.

> **The Lord bless you and keep you;**
> **The Lord make his face shine upon you**
> **and be gracious to you;**
> **The Lord turn his face toward**
> **you and give you peace.**
> **—Numbers 6:24-26**

CONCLUSION

I am the Lord who practices steadfast love, *justice*, and righteousness in the earth. For in these things I delight, declares the Lord.
—Jeremiah 9:24

We started this book-journey with a couple of foundational ideas, ideas we wanted to illustrate throughout these pages.

The first was the call to disrupt generational poverty through the mechanism of eradicating 3rd-grade illiteracy, addressing the reality that 34% of 4th-graders read below basic levels. Remember how our friend Ron Fairchild from the Campaign for Grade Level Reading explained it. He said:

> The Campaign's starting point is really about *disrupting generational poverty*. And the earliest and best predictor for whether and to what extent kids are going to succeed in school and life; *one of the best predictors we have is 3rd-grade reading proficiency.*

The second was an invitation to meet Jesus in fresh ways by participating in God's heart for the poor, forgotten, marginalized, and tossed aside.

Jesus said it:

Truly I tell you, whatever you did for one of the
least of these brothers and sisters
of mine, you did for me.
—Matthew 25:40

Bono, rock star and Jesus follower, was invited to speak at the 2006 U.S. National Prayer Breakfast in front of George W. Bush and hundreds of international dignitaries. He shared his heart on God's invitation. This is a sample of what he shared:

One thing we can all agree on, all faiths and ideologies, is that God is with the vulnerable and poor. It's not a coincidence that in the Scriptures, poverty is mentioned more than 2,100 times. It's not an accident. That's a lot of airtime.

God is in the slums, in the cardboard boxes where the poor play house . . . God is in the silence of a mother who has infected her child with a virus that will end both

CONCLUSION 227

their lives . . . God is in the cries heard under the rubble of war . . . God is in the debris of wasted opportunity and lives, **and God is with us if we are with them.**

Bono is echoing the prophetic imagination of Isaiah:

If you spend yourselves in behalf of the hungry
and satisfy the needs of the oppressed,
then your light will rise in the darkness,
and your night will become like the noonday.
The Lord will guide you always;
he will satisfy your needs in a sun-scorched land
and will strengthen your frame.
You will be like a well-watered garden,
like a spring whose waters never fail.
—Isaiah 58:10-11

That seems like a really great promise. You get to meet Jesus when you care for the marginalized and tossed aside, and as if that is not enough, the LORD promises to "guide you," "satisfy your needs," "strengthen your frame," and make you "a well-watered garden" whose "waters never fail."

In 1974, Mother Teresa of Calcutta was interviewed by Nodlaig McCarthy on Irish Television (you can find the entire interview on YouTube[47]). Throughout the conversation,

McCarthy marveled at the great sacrifice that Mother Teresa modeled, caring for 46,000 lepers. She invited the nun to encourage her audience to live in a similar way.

Mother Teresa did not. Instead, she simply invited everyone with these words:

> We are trying to bring that *love and peace and joy to our neighborhood* and to the street where we live in the town where we live. I think love begins at home.

> Think one person, one individual person, one person at a time, *we can serve only the one at a time.* We can only love one day at a time.

> Help somebody in their own family first and then help their next-door neighbor. *Vocation is our belonging to Christ.* The work is only a means to put our love for Christ into action. *The work is not my work. It is the work of us all. You and me. Because it is His work.*

Somewhere along the way, our hearts were captured and compelled by the unshackling work of literacy. We hope that your heart has already moved beyond these imperfect pages and instead heard the voice of the Savior inviting you to love your neighbors in ways you never have before.

If being a reading mentor is where you want to begin, we are here to help. If inviting your small group, your community, or your church to come with you, we are here to help.

The best place to start would be to visit: TEACHaKIDtoREAD.com

Mother Teresa said, "one person, one individual person, one person at a time." And as you love one at a time, one day at a time . . . and as your church loves one school at a time and one neighborhood at a time . . . and as we all together find renewed, activated love for the poor in spirit, for the least of these, and for the stranger along the road, we might just find ourselves right smack dab in the middle of the redemptive work of the Kingdom of God . . .

Let's practice Heaven today.

HOW TO GET INVOLVED

If you are a concerned individual, a church leader, a business leader, a community activist, or anyone else wanting **to get personally involved** in engaging, promoting, and transforming early childhood literacy in your area, please visit:

TEACHaKIDtoREAD.com

TEACH a KID to READ is built on a simple idea: through literacy, we can change the lives of the current generation—and generations to come. We can end the cycles of poverty, prison, and addiction that plague our most vulnerable and limit their potential. At TEACH a KID to READ, we are dedicated to providing support and literacy services to those in need by activating a cavalry of caring volunteers.

TEACH a KID to READ believes literacy is critical to the success of a child's life. We are on a mission to transform the landscape of literacy, one person at a time. We strive to help children, families, communities, and schools gain access to the resources they need to learn to read and succeed.

Other Literacy Resources:

If you want **to understand more** about the national issue of illiteracy, see the most up-to-date research, the statistics and the national movements in advocacy, we recommend you visit our friends at the Campaign for Grade Level reading at:

GradeLevelReading.net

If you are a faith leader—a denominational leader, a believing leader of a literacy nonprofit, a church leader, a faith-network leader, a believing literacy advocate, a writer/filmmaker/influencer, etc.—who is currently working in literacy *or* who wants to **become an influential player in the Faith and Literacy space**, come join the Faith and Literacy Collective at:

FaithAndLiteracy.com

ACKNOWLEDGMENTS

In the spring of 2023, Tony and I had a few dreams, all of which had been lingering on the back burner for some time. We wanted to produce a film drawing the entire country's attention to the epidemic of illiteracy in the U.S. Secretly however, as you read in this book, our greatest calling was to support and inspire a national movement around faith and literacy. So we asked ourselves, "How do we speak to our beloved, powerful and compassionate faith family?"

The first idea was that Tony and I should speak directly to people and communities of faith about the cause of early childhood literacy. So we wrote this book (in fairness to Tony, he wrote most of the book). If you love God, believe in the unique calling and potential of God's people, and if you embrace Jesus' invitation to *love your neighbor*... then we wrote this book for you.

The second idea was that we would initiate a gathering (which we did in November 2023) of the people we know who are both networked people of faith and also have made Early Childhood Literacy their life's work.

We would limit the gathering to a few dozen "friends." Miracles occurred. Thanks to our Board Chairman, David Austin, a famous old facility in Arlington became our meeting site. All but a few people we invited came (on their own dime). Without knowing it, we launched the first ever Faith and Literacy Collective.

And what we learned at this event is that we had the opportunity to serve and save the entire church by inviting them into this neighborly cause. That is why we wrote this book. Some people ask us, "Why should the church give its limited time, talent, and treasure in the cause of literacy?" to which we answer, "Throughout human history there has been no greater force for language creation, education, and literacy than the Christian peoples. It has been a mission that has animated our faith. Let it animate us again."

All our gratitude to the leaders of the Faith and Literacy Collective. They are the heroes of this story. If you want to join us, you will be joining them. Visit www.FaithAndLiteracy.org to learn more.

We also want to acknowledge our friends at Unanimous Media (UnanimousMedia.com) and their foundation, Eat. Learn. Play. (EatLearnPlay.org). Your partnership has changed everything about the potential of our faith and literacy initiative. Stephen and Ayesha Curry embraced this cause before they even heard of us,

ACKNOWLEDGMENTS

and we are now in the fight together. Thank you to Andy Peterson (docsology.co) and Kalyna Kutny for encouraging this relationship.

We thank Maryanna Young, Heather Goetter, Rachel Langaker, Mercy Sorich, and the rest of the team at Aloha Publishing (AlohaPublishing.com) who immediately saw the potential of this book and its message and put their creativity and enthusiasm behind it.

There are many more people who contributed their brilliance and stories to these pages. I know I will probably miss someone, but here it goes. Thank you for the Campaign for Grade Level Reading (GradeLevelReading.net) and the Annie E. Casey Foundation (AECF.org) for their excellent research and statistics that fueled and supported this work. Gratitude to Ron Fairchild (SmarterLearningGroup.com) and Dr. Donna Beegle (ComBarriers.com) whose teaching we quote directly. There are so many stories we collected. Some of the people who generously contributed their stories are: Doug Kempton, Stephanie Korteweg, Roy Chang, Marquis Fletcher, Herman Greene, SouthLake Church, and Dale McFerron.

The making of our award-winning documentary, *SENTENCED* (SentencedFilm.com), was a six-year labor of love and sweat. We want to thank Connor Martin and Mark Allen Johnson and the entire directorial and editorial team who all partnered with us in creating much of this book's content.

READ, the film *SENTENCED*, the Faith and Literacy Collective, TEACHaKIDtoREAD.com, and all the rest of the work is powered by our nonprofit—Children's Literacy Project (url below)—and CLP is powered by a handful of very generous donors who've been rooting for us, remained patient with us, and believed in us. You know who you are. Thank you!

If you are reading this, thank you. Welcome to the Faith and Literacy movement. May this 2,000-year mission of language and education continue and may you contribute your verse.

Jeff Martin

Founder & President

ChildrensLiteracyProject.org

ABOUT THE AUTHORS

Tony Kriz is a collector . . . of stories, of friends, of trails, and of vistas. He is a theologian, professor, award-winning author, international speaker, and filmmaker. His influence extends from Eastern Europe to Portland, Oregon, from Yale University to the Southern Baptists, conservative and progressive think-tanks alike. His books include *Neighbors and Wise Men* and *ALOOF*. Most recently he was a writer/producer of the *SENTENCED* documentary.

Tony is husband to Aimee, father to three courageous and creative boys, unofficial ambassador of his beloved Portland, devoted to his neighborhood, loyal to his diverse communities, and a friend to the religious and irreligious alike. He is the Theological/Creative Director of TEACH a KID to READ.

Jeff Martin is a producer of award-winning, high-impact and culture-changing films including *SENTENCED*, *Undivided*, *A River Runs Between Us*, and *Lord, Save Us From Your Followers*. Jeff is the founder of Children's

Literacy Project and TEACH a KID to READ, organizations that inspire and activate churches, organizations, and individuals to bring much-needed resources and volunteers to our most at-risk public schools.

Jeff has been married to the love of his life since 1982. He has three wildly creative children and six grandchildren who constantly invade his home. He loves his garden, his family, his friends, his church, and this work in literacy. His first career was running a large creative firm. His dynamic life has been the best preparation for his second act: animating and activating communities into a movement that cares for all of God's children.

ENDNOTES

1. https://online.regiscollege.edu/blog/child-illiteracy/
2. https://www.aecf.org/blog/low-reading-scores-show-majority-of-us-children-not-prepared-for-future-s#:~:text=-Casey%20Foundation%20finds%20that%2080,future%20educational%20and%20economic%20success.
3. https://www.chicagotribune.com/2013/02/19/prison-data-court-files-show-link-between-school-truancy-and-crime/#:~:text=Of%20182%20boys%20and%20young,when%20they%20were%20booked%20in.
4. https://www.usatoday.com/story/news/education/2023/09/09/literacy-levels-in-the-us/70799429007/
5. https://online.regiscollege.edu/blog/child-illiteracy/
6. Ashton, K., A.R. Davies, K. Hughes, et al. "Adult Support During Childhood: A Retrospective Study of Trusted Adult Relationships, Sources of Personal Adult Support and Their Association with Childhood Resilience Resources." BMC Psychology 9, no. 101 (2021). https://doi.org/10.1186/s40359-021-00601-x.
7. https://www.youtube.com/watch?v=q-OkJ3Kq56g
8. https://www.aecf.org/blog/fourth-grade-reading-proficiency-2022

9. https://nces.ed.gov/pubsearch/pubsinfo.asp?pubid=2021025

10. Randazzo, Sara, and Scott Calvert. "More States Threaten to Hold Back Third-Graders Who Can't Read," *The Wall Street Journal*, August 17, 2023. https://www.wsj.com/us-news/education/more-states-threaten-to-hold-back-third-graders-who-cant-read-19f9765

11. https://www.aecf.org/blog/poverty-puts-struggling-readers-in-double-jeopardy-minorities-most-at-risk and https://www.aecf.org/resources/double-jeopardy

12. https://www.ccf.ny.gov/files/9013/8262/2751/AECFReporReadingGrade3.pdf

13. https://www.ccf.ny.gov/files/9013/8262/2751/AECFReporReadingGrade3.pdf

14. https://www.firstthingsfirst.org/early-childhood-matters/brain-development/#:~:text=90%25%20of%20Brain%20Growth%20Happens,full%20grown%20%E2%80%93%20by%20age%205.

15. https://www.ncbi.nlm.nih.gov/books/NBK525261/#:~:text=Developmental%20Trajectories%20of%20Brain%20Morphometry,percent%20of%20its%20adult%20volume.

16. https://www.samhsa.gov/child-trauma/understanding-child-trauma

17. https://www.samhsa.gov/child-trauma/understanding-child-trauma#:~:text=More%20than%20two%20thirds%20of,Community%20or%20school%20violence

18. https://news.harvard.edu/gazette/story/2020/08/violence-and-trauma-in-childhood-accelerate-puberty/

19. https://developingchild.harvard.edu/science/key-concepts/serve-and-return/

20. https://usafacts.org/articles/how-many-us-children-receive-a-free-or-reduced-price-school-lunch/

21. https://schoolnutrition.org/about-school-meals/school-meal-statistics/

22. https://www.literacyforallfund.org/facts#:~:text=Of%20adults%20with%20the%20lowest,educational%20scores%20and%20higher%20earnings.

23. https://www.ncbi.nlm.nih.gov/pmc/articles/PMC10118140/ and https://www.cbp.gov/border-security/human-trafficking

24. https://www.ncbi.nlm.nih.gov/pmc/articles/PMC3606637/#:~:text=Results,CI%3A%201.67%2D3.77).

25. https://www.chicagotribune.com/2013/02/19/prison-data-court-files-show-link-between-school-truancy-and-crime/#:~:text=Of%20182%20boys%20and%20young,when%20they%20were%20booked%20in.

26. Williamson, G. LaVerne. "Education and Incarceration: An Examination of the Relationship Between Educational Achievement and Criminal Behavior," *Journal of Correctional Education* 43:1 (March 1992).

27. National Center for Education Statistics: https://nces.ed.gov/

28. https://www.sentencingproject.org/

29. https://developingchild.harvard.edu/science/key-concepts/resilience/

30. https://www.bls.gov/oes/current/oes111011.htm

31. https://meridian.allenpress.com/jmr/article/109/2/13/494447/FSMB-Census-of-Licensed-Physicians-in-the-United

32. https://www.dailykos.com/stories/2015/3/29/1372225/-Just-how-many-elected-officials-are-there-in-the-United-States-The-answer-is-mind-blowing

33. https://www.forbes.com/advisor/retirement/how-many-billionaires-and-millionaires-live-in-the-u-s/

34. https://worldpopulationreview.com/country-rankings/phd-percentage-by-country

35. https://research.com/universities-colleges/number-of-public-schools-in-the-us

36. https://nces.ed.gov/fastfacts/display.asp?id=372#:~:text=How%20many%20teachers%20were%20there,in%20private%20schools%20(source).

37. Annual education spending for 2019-2020: https://www.edweek.org/policy-politics/what-america-spends-on-k-12-the-latest-federal-snapshot/2022/05#:~:text=America%20invested%20%24795%20billion%20in,school%20spending%20data%20released%20Wednesday.

38. https://www.barbarabush.org/wp-content/uploads/2020/09/BBFoundation_GainsFromEradicatingIlliteracy_9_8.pdf and also see: https://www.apmresearchlab.org/10x-adult-literacy

39. https://www.theedadvocate.org/5-fascinating-statistics-about-high-school-dropouts-in-america/

40. https://repository.library.northeastern.edu/downloads/neu:376324 and https://www.graduationalliance.com/2017/03/06/the-true-cost-of-high-school-dropouts/#:~:text=Half%20of%20Americans%20on%20public,nearly%20%24957%20BILLION%20a%20year.

41. https://nces.ed.gov/fastfacts/display.asp?id=16

42. https://nces.ed.gov/programs/coe/pdf/coe_cnb.pdf
43. National Research Council (1998). *Preventing Reading Difficulties in Young Children.* Edited by C. Snow, S. Burns, and P. Griffin, Committee on the Prevention of Reading Difficulties in Young Children. Washington, DC: National Academy Press. https://nap.nationalacademies.org/catalog/6023/preventing-reading-difficulties-in-young-children
44. https://mcc.gse.harvard.edu/reports/loneliness-in-america
45. https://www.hhs.gov/sites/default/files/surgeon-general-social-connection-advisory.pdf
46. https://agsjournals.onlinelibrary.wiley.com/doi/10.1111/jgs.18140 and https://www.hopkinsmedicine.org/news/newsroom/news-releases/2023/01/new-studies-suggest-social-isolation-is-a-risk-factor-for-dementia-in-older-adults-point-to-ways-to-reduce-risk
47. https://www.youtube.com/watch?v=Th2QzJwy8tI and https://www.youtube.com/watch?v=FF5n4HScSP4, for example

ChildrensLiteracyProject.org